TAKE 6 CARROTS, 4 HEADS OF CELERY, 8 LARGE ONIONS ...

Maya Pieris

TAKE 6 CARROTS,

4 HEADS OF CELERY,

8 LARGE ONIONS ...

The Receipts of a Hertfordshire Family

edited and adapted for the

modern kitchen

by

MAYA PIERIS

HITCHIN HISTORICAL SOCIETY

Hitchin Historical Society, Hitchin, Hertfordshire, England

First published 1994

Copyright © Maya Pieris and Hitchin Historical Society

ISBN 0 9512109 1 2

British Library Cataloguing - in - Publication Data

A catalogue record for this book is available from the British Library

TYPESET IN TIMES NEW ROMAN BY MAYA PIERIS AND JOHN MAHONEY

PRINTED IN ENGLAND BY

STREETS PRINTERS LIMITED

BALDOCK, HERTFORDSHIRE

Contents

This book is dedicated to all Hitchin worthies,

past, present and future

Foreword

One of the best ways to become acquainted with people is through food and drink and the following recipes provide just this opportunity. They allow us a glimpse into the personal lives of the Wilsheres, a typical wealthy nineteenth century family some of whose members I have attempted to 'sketch', to add a little flesh to the bones of the people who would have sampled these recipes.

Much of the impetus for the book has been due to the Hitchin British Schools' project which is currently seeking to restore the nineteenth century school buildings in the town to create a living museum. The Wilsheres were very closely associated with the founding and running of the school and, along with Lord Dacre, the other founding father, are remembered in the successor school named Wilshere-Dacre.

Further impetus has come from my own particular interest in historical cookery. The opportunity to work with an original document has been most enjoyable and informative, historically and gastronomically!

To quote Mrs.Beeton '*I must frankly own, that if I had known, beforehand, that this book would have cost me the labour which it has, I should never have been courageous enough to commence it.*' (1) And my effort is paltry in comparison! The project has, however, taken me a lot longer to see to fruition and many thanks must go to the following people and organisations who have helped me in various ways. Firstly to Scilla Douglas who has been a great support as a friend and experienced author; to Alison Taylor, curator of Hitchin Museum, Martin Roberts and Cynthia Hindmarch, also from the museum, who had fun, I hope, in helping me decipher the recipes and generally locating relevant material; to David Howlett and other committee members of the Hitchin Historical Society for their advice; to Lesley Clarke, Linda Tobey, Pauline Humphries and Peggy Pieris for helping to trial the recipes; to Bridget Howlett and Karen Stokes for reading the manuscript; to the staff at the Hertfordshire County Records Office and the Hertfordshire Local Studies Service; to the following for permission to quote from published and private documents: Mr.W.A.Wright; Tony Rook; SmithKline Beecham; Hawkins Russell Jones; to all the many other friends and acquaintances who have taken a friendly interest and listened to me 'boring' on about the project; to my husband, John, who provided practical, professional help and lots of loving support even when the recipes went wrong; and to Ursula, aged 21 months, who put up with being ignored when mum was busy!

An aerial view of the historic heart of Hitchin taken in 1957 clearly showing the central mediaeval infill, originally a large open market area.

Introduction

Travel a mere 35 minutes north from Kings Cross on the train and you come to Hitchin, a small north Hertfordshire market town. Its nearest urban neighbours, ever closer, are Stevenage and Luton with Letchworth, the first Garden City, just to the north. The town lies, therefore, near to the borders with Bedfordshire and Cambridgeshire, the Chilterns on its westerly edge with the low, flat panorama of these counties to the north and east. It is an area of much antiquity with pre-Roman settlements such as that at Hexton and evidence for the presence of King Offa at Offley. The Icknield Way also passes close by, linking the area with other sites of ancient habitation in southern England.

Hitchin itself is a good example of the classic English market town epitomised by such places as Ludlow in Shropshire. It is a place that has developed over many centuries, growing around the old church, which in 1992 celebrated 1200 years as a place of worship, and the priory which passed into private ownership in the sixteenth century. The town centre remains largely intact architecturally, maps and aerial views clearly showing the original early medieval market configuration. The twentieth century has, however, not passed by without some effects upon the town and not always satisfactorily. Old and new do, though, attempt positive relationships and Hitchin continues an architectural gem in North Hertfordshire.

As with other similar towns Hitchin is a place where certain family names crop up over the decades and centuries, commemorated in places or frequently road names, the Wilsheres and Lord Dacre, the British Schools' co-founder, in the school Wilshere-Dacre. Other established Hitchin names continue in various retail establishments such as Gatwards, the jewellers, and Hawkins, haberdashers. It is this element of civic continuity that has been largely responsible for the continued thriving of the town over so many centuries and which will serve it well in years to come.

One of the family's memorial tablets from St Mary's Church, Welwyn commemorating some of the earlier family members. Note how constantly the names 'William', 'Thomas' and 'John' are used. (See Family Tree)

Chapter One

The Family Album

The Wilsheres are a good example of that Victorian social group - the philanthropic upper middle class, energetic with a keen interest in local affairs, not particularly glamorous but forming the backbone of many nineteenth century towns. They were one of the wealthier families in Hitchin, among those '*most prominent in Hitchin business and Hitchin life in the late eighteenth and early nineteenth centuries*' along with such families as the Lucases and Ransomes. (1) Census records also show, however, a number of poorer working class families bearing the name Wilshere with variations such as 'Wilshire' and 'Wilsher'. The name continues to be a fairly common local occurrence.

They were, however, also a family with a historical pedigree, local minor gentry recorded as living in the Welwyn area, at The Frythe, from the fifteenth century though the name is believed to be a variant of 'Wiltshire', the '*regional name from the county of Wiltshire*'(2). This may well surprise Hitchin residents as there is an assumption that the family is very much a Hitchin 'product'. The documentation shows, however, that it was originally a Welwyn family maintaining strong and constant links with that place from the earliest days. The nineteenth century Wilsheres retained close domestic links with The Frythe, with the family moving back there during the lifetime of Charles Willes Wilshere and maintaining residence there till the property was eventually sold in the 1950s.

The evidence, however, tells us that the Wilsheres, or Wylsheres, can be traced back to the fourteenth century to the time of Richard II as living in Welwyn where they were yeoman farmers and innkeepers. Here they leased the Frythe estate, part of the possession of the Convent of Holywell. The name 'Frythe' indicates a greater antiquity dating back to Saxon times though no specific mention occurs in the Domesday Book. The Old English word '(ge)fyrho' indicated an area of wooded land rather than a particular property. (3) The earliest reference to the place occurs in a document dated 1260 which refers to land deals involving a John del Frith. The Wilsheres' involvement, however, dates from 1523 when a William Wylshere signed a sixty year lease for property described as 'a *tenement called the Boreshede and another tenement called Frithe which standeth in a felde called Grigges Felde*' (4). Presumably the 'Boreshede' was a hostelry perhaps indicating an interest in brewing that some later generations also had.

On the dissolution of the monasteries the land was granted to the Gostwicks with the Wilsheres remaining as tenants. In 1546 William Gostwick sold the estate to William Wilshere now referred to as a 'gentleman'. This William showed the civic concern that characterised later generations in a bequest '*to the mendynge of the highways betwixt Welwyn towne and Holmer Hill leading to The Frythe the sum of ten shillings*' (5).

The family seemed to prosper with the memorial tablets in St. Mary's Church, Welwyn showing them to be wealthy men. They were, in fact, generous patrons of the church and in the nineteenth century undertook a radical remodelling and rebuilding of the church not to everyone's taste as it was to '*obscure every trace of the original structure*' (6). The church and other properties in and around Welwyn village contain examples of chronograms devised by the Wilsheres. Chronograms combine an inscription and a date picked out in the capital letters and to be read as Roman numerals, a complicated pastime! The following appears on the gable ends of the side chapel.

SIBI.ET.PAROCHIANIS.HAEC.CHORI.ALA.DE.SVO

CVRA.CAROLI.WILLES.WILSHERE.CONDITA.EST

The meaning and date are as follows.

'This choir aisle of his responsibility was built by Charles Willes

Wilshere for himself and the parish.'

1+1   +100+1+1   +100+100+1+50+500+5

+100+5+100+50+1+1+50+50+1+50   +100+500+1 = 1869

The family habit of using the names 'William' and 'John' was established early as can be seen from the family tree. With the earlier generations, to quote Cussons, *'the individuality of each is therefore difficult to determine'*(7). William was traditionally the name of the eldest son. One William bought the manors of Much Hadham and Great Wymondley which included the right to hand the Monarch the first cup of wine at the Coronation Banquet, a right last claimed at the banquet of George IV. (8)

The estate continued a family possession though not always inhabited by them. Pigot's Provincial and Commercial Directory of 1832 lists a R.Perrot Esq. as living at The Frythe with the 1839 edition listing a Clutterbuck Esq. Not a lot is recorded about the women of the family though their names appear in various censuses recorded as living at the same dwellings. In the postscript to Tony Rook's booklet on the church, however, the then rector Terence Wenham recalled the following incident involving the three sisters of Charles Willes Wilshere. *'The late Cecil Hollingsworth told me that, when he was a footman at The Frythe, he once answered a knock at the imposing front entrance . "It is the Rector," he informed the three Misses Wilshere, who were sitting in the drawing room. "Tell the Rector we are not at home," he was instructed.'* (9) One possible reason for this 'coolness' can be found in a chronogram on Homerswood Cottage, Digswell Hill built in 1874.

ECCLESIAE PAROCHIALIS AMPLIFICATIO RECTOR ET

POPVLO PROPOSITA NON PLACVIT

(Erected in) a year in which the proposed extension to the

parish church was not pleasing to the rector and the people. (10)

Furthermore the Misses Wilshere had their own key to the church entering by the door, now gone, to the Frythe Chapel. Obviously strong views were held by the family. It is hard, therefore, to imagine the ladies of the family being anything other than similarly strong-minded and active in civic ventures but no particular evidence of their activities has come to light.

The Wilshere coat of arms described as 'party cheveronwise azure and or with six crosslets or in the chief with a lion rampant as the crest.' Their motto was 'fidelis'.

A portrait of William Wilshere founder of the Hitchin British Schools and friend and adviser to Samuel Whitbread the brewer. Probably painted circa 1810.

Chapter 2

The Hitchin Wilsheres

William Wilshere (1754-1824)

Most evidence for the link between Hitchin and the Wilsheres dates from the turn of the eighteenth century with a William Wilshere born in 1754. His grandfather, also William, had owned a brewery in the town and was succeeded by a son, again William. This William had been a deacon in the Queen Street Independent Chapel, which highlights an area of diverse thinking within the family with certain members choosing to practise their Christianity outside the structure of the established church. William continued in the family business as a maltster but lacked a certain business acumen though throughout *'all his difficulties he retained some hold upon the little farm at The Frythe'* (1). He was also fortunate that Elizabeth Simpson, a benefactress in the town and a distant relation left him her Bancroft property and other lands and money which were to form his children's inheritance. Following the failure of his business, William found employment with Richard Tristram in his Portmill Lane legal practice helping with the various stewardships. His first son, born in 1754, was named William in accordance with the family's tradition and was the eldest of 14 children many of whom died in infancy or early adulthood. William, however, survived the many dangers of infancy and became one of the town's major benefactors and perhaps the best known member of his family, in the words of Francis Lucas, a fellow Hitchinite, *'the most remarkable of a very remarkable family'*. (2)

He resided *'in the house in Bancroft behind the Chestnut trees'* according to Lucas though the inventory at death of his property does not specify a property. (3) The addresses given with the recipes include 109 Bancroft and the Croft, also in Bancroft, so it is possible that he was also resident at one or both of these. Hine also makes mention of the Hermitage in his documentation. The inventory describes a property of some size which could refer to any of these properties. Poole and Fleck in their book on Hitchin recall how William would *'each summer... send a basket of strawberries and cauliflowers to Dr. Niblock at the Free School to exemplify that judicious mixture of utility and luxury which he, as a trustee, felt should be maintained in the curriculum'*. (4) By profession a lawyer he was described in the Universal British Directory of 1794 as an 'attorney' becoming the head of the firm which eventually became Hawkins and Co., now Hawkins Russell Jones. His clients included several of the local landowners and gentry, in particular Samuel Whitbread the brewer. He was, in fact a close friend and financial adviser to Whitbread who lived relatively near by in Cardington and loaned substantial amounts to the brewer. The Whitbreads appear to have been distant relatives, an earlier John Wilshere having married Dorothy, daughter of William Whitbread of Cardington in 1686. This may well account for Wilshere's close involvement with Whitbread's business. William was not a man to waste his time and money. Hine, in his unfinished history of the solicitors' firm, records that William was a tough and enterprising business man known as 'Devil' Wilshere on account of his willingness to lend money but also to foreclose where necessary. (5)

15

William was also involved in the creation of the Hitchin Militia. He is reputed to have said, when informed of the difficulty in providing arms for the men, that '....*If we cannot get muskets then, by God we shall fight them with pikes. We fought them with pikes in days gone by, we will do so again*'. (6) According to Hine the French Revolution concerned William enough for him to have a secret chamber created in his house. Whether this was the Bancroft or Hermitage property is a little unclear from Hine's writings. (7)

William also purchased the Manor of Great Wymondley and was the last person to perform the task of handing the first cup of wine to the monarch, George IV, at the coronation banquet. The cup was traditionally given to the bearer as a fee and not surprisingly became a family heirloom. As 'Lord of the Manor' William applied his legal and business mind to a precise description of the manor boundaries though strangely this was not recorded on a map.

Though a wealthy man William appears to have suffered various fluctuations in his personal fortunes as can be seen from the records of his deposits with Pierson's Bank. In 1805 he had a deposit of £7,019 which rose to £32,427 in 1810 and by 1811 had fallen to £28,497. 8) At his death in 1824 the inventory of his household goods amounted to £5.644,12,6 with the cellar value totalling £1173,15. (9) Foster states that between 1812 and 1824 the balance fluctuated between £17,000 and £6,215. (10) Such was his wealth, however, that at one time he was able to lend Samuel Whitbread the astonishing amount of £80,000, worth some millions by today's prices. Shrewdly his arrangement was to take a future share of the profits which according to his family '*produced him a clear annual income of £10,000*' , a lot of money! (11)

Probably the most important civic project that he was involved in was the founding of the British Schools in Queen Street, undertaken in conjunction with his friend Thomas Brand, later Lord Dacre. His involvement with the scheme stemmed from his acquaintance with Samuel Whitbread though William and a sister had already made contributions to a Hitchin Sunday school. Whitbread knew Joseph Lancaster, the inspiration behind the British Schools movement and introduced the idea to Wilshere. In 1810 he and Thomas Brand endowed a foundation for boys, the girls' school coming nearly 10 years later. In his will William left various monies and land to the town including the school which was handed over to its trustees in 1826. According to an account of the Hitchin Charities in a commissioners' report of 1833 William had left £500 towards the Free School founded by John Mattocke for the '*greatest permanent benefit to the poor of Hitchin*'. (12) In 1827 the trustees and executors had agreed a division of £200 to increase the mistress's salary of the girls' charity school in Portmill Lane and £300 for the master's salary of the Tilehouse boys' free school with the proviso that 10 more girls and 10 more boys were admitted.

William was given to the recording of details, perhaps as a result of his legal training, particularly of matters concerning himself. Branch Johnson, in a highly entertaining and informative article entitled 'The Vital Statistics of Mr.Wilshere', describes how William

The Croft in Bancroft, Hitchin about 1866. The view shows this imposing property abutting a busy market street as shown by the animal pens.

This second view of the Croft, also about 1866, was taken from the rear and presents a much more elegant and refined prospect.

recorded in his private notebooks minute details of his weight and girth. From this can be drawn a mental picture of a man of Pickwickian stature who at age 43 weighed a little over 14 stone, his girth measuring 3ft 6½in. (13) William died in 1824 and according to Hine was much mourned. He recalls William Lucas's diary entry which said '*This day died William Wilshere, the most eminent public character of this town and neighbourhood; a man of great prudence & sagacity, who, as attorney & steward of many copyhold manors, acquired much wealth & influence. A very kind friend to the poor.*' (14) He was a man with a great sense of civic duty who contributed to national debates on matters such as the Poor Laws, giving evidence to the 1817 Lords Committee, and was a friend and acquaintance of such reformers as Howard and Wilberforce but he was not a man to court popularity for its own sake. He sagaciously observed that '*lasting popularity is seldom sudden: sudden popularity is seldom lasting.*' (15) His wife had died many years before and there had been no child. William had never remarried. He arranged, therefore, to name his brother Thomas's son William as his heir.

John (1755-1836) and Thomas Wilshere (1775-1832)

These two, William's brothers, are listed in the Hertfordshire Directory of 1826/7 as one of the gentry with John further listed as a corn/seed and wine merchant and a maltster. John had a reputation as something of an eccentric. William Lucas described him as the '*most singular and original character in our town*'. (16) His son, yet again William, was described by Francis Lucas as '*a man of very odd habits*' who apparently '*Sat up all night and lay in bed most of the day. He sometimes showed himself in the daytime but never on foot.*' (17) Also an astute business man John had a reputation for meanness described by Lucas as '*wonderfully parsimonious*'. (18) In his article on the Wilsheres Basham recalls the description of him as '*dressed in a very old, broad-rimmed white hat and an equally old, drab box coat, which he buttoned across his chest without putting his arms in the sleeves.*' (19)

There was apparently no love between William and John and according to Francis Lucas the latter '*would lose no opportunity of holding him up to ridicule or even execration, though never allowing anyone else to say a word against him.*' (20) Apparently relations became so strained that William felt obliged to file a formal complaint against John which '*craved sureties of the peace.*' (21) At William's funeral he is even rumoured to have cheered as though pleased.

John was apparently very fond of a '*rice pudding made with eggs very sweet and thoroughly baked, over which he would pour a little of his choicest sherry.*' (22) The specific recipe does not occur in the collection though there is a baked egg pudding to be served with a wine sauce.

The 1832 Hertfordshire Directory lists Thomas along with a Mary and Ann Wilshere as living in Bancroft with William and a Laura Wilshere resident at the Hermitage.

An interior view of the Croft, over one hundred years ago, showing how ornate it must have been. Regrettably the building was demolished in the 1960s.

A view of the extensive gardens of the Hermitage which gave both its name and land to Hermitage Road in Hitchin. The grounds give some indication of the size and status of this property which dated back to medieval times.

According to Hine this apparently quiet, sober man was inspired to purchase for £1500 *'the good ship James of 300 tons... fitted with all speed for a Privateer against the French'.* The ship indulged in nothing less than piracy against th French at a time when we were not yet at war with them and after some 'success' was captured by them. Perhaps not surprisingly this behaviour led to a rift with the upstanding William. (23) Unlike his two brothers Thomas was not a natural business man though he found some success in the insurance business as an agent for a Sir Francis Willes. Though no firm evidence has been found for the following it seems possible that this is the origin of Charles Willes Wilshere's middle name. Thomas died in a freak accident when the horses pulling his open carriage returning from a funeral were frightened by some plough horses running about in Grays Lane and Thomas was thrown out. (24) Like many of his immediate family he was buried in the graveyard of the town's Independent Chapel.

William Wilshere (1804-1867)

He was the eldest son of Thomas and heir to his uncle William's estates. His uncle had great expectations of William and to some extent groomed him for the political life that had never been his. The nephew continued the family tradition of service and became an M.P. and High Sheriff of Hertfordshire. In the Post Office Directory of 1846 he is listed amongst the gentry described as an MP (for Great Yarmouth) residing at the Hermitage. During his time The Frythe was rebuilt on the site of the earlier building, the result being a substantial dwelling. Money was lavishly spent on items such as a 'Mahogany Patent Bath' costing £5-10-0 and on ironmongery quoted at £458-8-11.(25)

William also owned substantial pieces of land in Hitchin including land in Grays Lane and Mount Pleasant. He also continued to support the British Schools in Queen Street and was further involved in the founding of another such school in Walsworth, Hitchin, giving the land and an annual guarantee of £5. (26)

 He died whilst in Paris and, being unmarried, was succeeded by his younger brother Charles. Less driven than his uncle, William was, nonetheless, a man with a civic conscience and a man who had some personal popularity. In the press obituary he was described as someone who, ironically, *'had but little political ambition'*, who *'never sought or cared for such distinctions.....There are some men who have qualities which compel our respect, but who never inspire our love. Mr.Wilshere was not one of these.'* (27)

William Wilshere, the nephew of the elder William, who was groomed for a political life but was by nature a somewhat shy and retiring man. Circa 1860.

Charles Willes Wilshere 1814-1906

He lived at various locations in Hitchin including Bancroft House before moving to The Frythe in Welwyn. The 1851 census lists him as aged 37 and resident in Bancroft along with his wife, Elizabeth Marie aged 40, and daughters Edith Elizabeth Marie aged 9, Everlida Frances aged 4, Florence aged 3 and Alice Augusta aged 10 months. Florence was born in Florence hence her name. She was the only daughter to marry but died shortly after giving birth to a boy, Sydney, who died some 16 months later.

Charles was also closely involved in town interests and was a JP, a Deputy Lieutenant of the county and a Trustee of the Hitchin Charities. He, too, was concerned with the education of the townspeople and gave land in Hollow Lane for the establishment of the original St. Andrew/s School. He also purchased a chapel known as Bull's Barn and had it converted into St. John the Baptist Mission Church and donated land in Walsworth for the building of St. Faith's Church. Other land deals included the sale of the Nettledell Estate which formed the site of Highbury Road, The Avenue and Chiltern Road. He was also closely involved in the life of Welwyn where he did much to renovate and change the church, not always to everyone's taste, and also indulged his interest in chronograms.

Charles was effectively the last Wilshere to have any influence in Hitchin. By the time of his death, at the grand old age of 92, he was living at The Frythe in Welwyn. His estate passed to his surviving spinster daughters, the last of whom, Alice, died in 1934. The estate then passed to her great nephew, Gerald Maunsell Farmer, who had to adopt the name 'Wilshere' under the terms of the will. He and a friend opened The Frythe as a hotel, 'The Frythe Residential Private Hotel'. It was a flourishing business until the property was suddenly commissioned for war use, reputedly to do with the secret services. (28) The estate was finally wound up with the sale of The Frythe to ICI in 1955, the present owners being SmithKline Beecham.

This saw the end of one of the county's oldest families. Much evidence of the family still remains in Welwyn especially in the church and in Hitchin in such places as Wilshere-Dacre School and the Frythe Cottages while the British Schools' project also serves to remind us of the contributions of this Hertfordshire family.

Charles Willes Wilshere from a drawing by the Hitchin artist Samuel Lucas and dated 1857.

A view of The Frythe, Welwyn, in the 1870's following the extensive remodelling by Charles' elder brother William. The house is now part of the SmithKline Beecham complex.

Chapter 3

Food and cooking : a nineteenth century context

The Wilshere recipes occupy a time of much culinary change; changes in techniques; in etiquette; in availability of foods through changes in farming techniques and trade; and in the development of processed and packaged foods. Many of today's household names such as Crosse & Blackwell and Lea & Perrins were the culinary success stories of their day though we would not necessarily recognise these Victorian manufacturers and retailers in today's producers. Until the last quarter of the century preparation remained largely by hand - today a mark of quality - and so on a comparatively small scale. In 1854 Lea & Perrins output per day was 1,000 bottles. The only mechanical aid was a hand operated grinder, the sauce being mixed and bottled manually. Of course the market was still small for manufactured goods. The legion poor certainly could not afford such items. By the 1890s, however, a typical middle-class cook's store cupboard would have contained an array of packets, cans and bottles. Indeed in her book 'A Year's Cookery' dated 1895, Phyllis Browne, one of dozens of enthusiastic cookery writers, makes liberal use of a variety of prepared foods from tinned mushrooms to tinned potted grouse.

This time was also one of great social change and upheaval with appalling levels of poverty and so malnutrition amongst the working classes. In her book on Victorian food 'Mutton and Oysters' Sarah Freeman cites instances of the trade in second-hand food where the leftovers from the tables of the great and good were sold to the poor. Apparently the shopkeeper concerned was also a pig keeper and in this role collected the kitchen rubbish from some of the London clubs and local lunatic asylums. He obviously had the 'bright' idea of availing the local poor of such delicacies with his window display looking '*as though the fragments of a hundred feasts were here gathered*'. Perhaps not surprisingly the clientele was less enthusiastic about the offerings from the asylums. The Victorian entrepreneurial spirit at its most cynical. (1) Alexis Soyer, the great chef, was one of an increasing number concerned with the levels of poverty and nutrition amongst the working classes and headed a public subscription for soup kitchens for the poor. Charles Francatelli, cook to Queen Victoria, was also keen to express his concern for the undernourished underclasses and in 1861 published a volume entitled 'A Plain Cookery Book for the Working Classes'. In the book he exhorts the poor to '*strive to lay by a little of your weekly wage to purchase ... things*' (1) This did not stop him, however, from including a copious recipe for brewing your own beer. Interestingly some of these recipes provide examples of the growing influence of processed foods in the use of Brown and Polson cornflour for use in 'Brown and Polson Pudding'. (2)

The period was also one which saw the emergence amongst the middle and upper classes of a greater interest in and concern with food, its production, preparation, quality and presentation. The poor, as ever, took what they could get. Interest in animal husbandry had been developing in the previous century and had resulted in extreme examples of large,

"To market, to market to buy a fat pig". A drawing by Samuel Lucas of pigs at Smithfield market done about 1850.

obese animals. The Victorian preference was for a leaner animal though still fat by current standards. It is during this period that British beef developed its reputation for quality, one which it still maintains, almost becoming a national symbol. Mutton also continued to be a popular meat as can be seen from the numerous recipes for it. Pigs tended to be reared on a more domestic scale with many people keeping at least one and that often in close proximity to family members. Sarah Freeman cites an example of an old couple who kept a pig under the stairs, the wife even knitting it a jumper. (3) As late as 1906 the Hitchin Inspector of Nuisances was called upon to deal with the somewhat odiferous problems associated with such intimate pig husbandry such as the complaint received '*of pigs being kept so as to cause a nuisance. I found the pigs premises very clean but the hot weather certainly did make them smell strong.*'(4) A further cause for concern was noted a year later relating to a bakehouse '*dark and dirty and plastered ceiling falling down. The out buildings require limewashing and the stable and pigstye require drainage and the floor repairing.*' (5)

Vegetable consumption remained limited, little appreciated for the vitamin and fibre values, the study of such chemical matters being in its infancy. According to Drummond and Wilbraham by the nineteenth century the '*custom of ruining good vegetables by boiling them was established.*' (6) Indeed one recipe for cooking peas suggests a stewing time of some two hours. The landed gentry with their huge walled fruit and vegetable gardens undoubtedly had greater access to a wide variety of produce dependant upon a veritable army of gardeners and ultimately kitchen staff. The two regimes have been well documented in Jennifer Davies' two books on Victorian kitchen gardens and kitchens. (See bibliography)

Cooking methods also underwent gradual changes, at least in the homes of the middle classes upwards. Open hearths gave way to the closed iron ranges which seem to us to represent the archetypal Victorian kitchen, almost a celebration of the wonders of industrialisation that were helping to improve the lives of some. They would have been coal-fired, gas cookers only gaining popularity from the 1880s. Oven roasting, however, took some time to catch on with many continuing to prefer the 'barbecued' flavour of spit roasted meat. The development at the beginning of the century of the Dutch or reflector oven did much to ease the spit roasting approach by placing the joint in a concave iron or tin reflecting screen in front of the fire with access for basting the joint from the back. The poor, if lucky, might have had access to such devices but otherwise would have continued to cook in the more old fashioned and limiting methods. As for kitchen implements there were some early examples of gadgetry such as the tin opener, vital as canning developed, and the potato peeler while pots and pans changed shape to flatter bottomed, shorter handled objects more suited to a range. Cast iron and tin plate also became increasingly used in preference to copper and brass which required arduous cleaning to keep them safe to use. Verdigris poisoning was not that uncommon. Refrigeration was also developing during this period both as a domestic aid and as a means of preserving and thus exporting perishable goods from the colonies.

This culinary interest and concern can also be seen in the gradual growth from the middle of the eighteenth century in cookery publications, creating a new literary tradition and perhaps also heralding the demise of the more local, oral traditions. Traditional recipes became increasingly formalised with recipes for the first time containing specific and standardised information. Mrs Beeton remains one of the best known of these media successes. She was, though, but one of many nineteenth century cookery writers who also included Eliza Acton and Mrs Rundell, perhaps more worthy of culinary merit.

An invoice from Gatwards for various hardware items including a birdcage and dated 1852. Gatwards are still in business in Hitchin, well known for their jewellery business.

Chapter 4

The Wilshere Collection

The recipes do not present a picture of a grand family particularly given to entertaining in the elaborate style of a Francatelli or a Soyer. They are of a rather more domestic and functional nature, often provided by other persons, presumably friends or relations. Given the Wilsheres' social status, however, it is also likely that they would have entertained in a grander culinary style on some occasions. A quick examination of the elder William's wines and spirits inventory clearly shows a man interested in his liquid refreshments and these would have demanded more formal menus. It is also worth noting that he spent most of his life as a widower. Presumably he entertained not infrequently.

The responsibility for the recipes is ascribed to the two Williams and Charles Willes Wilshere though it is unlikely that these three gentlemen were actually the authors. This attribution occurs on a loose cover to the documents that was probably penned by Reginald Hine. No other evidence is available to further define authorship. It is more likely that the various female relations were responsible for the collection.

The fact that two generations of Wilsheres are cited indicates a span of time from the early nineteenth century to the end of it. It is possible to date the collection to 1824, the date on the recipe for the Vermicelli Pudding and also the year of the elder William's death, but many of the recipes will date from an earlier time. A strong oral tradition still existed though the rapid development of the printed media would soon displace this.

The collection is formed of separate sheets rather than a bound document and so is random in its construction. There are recipes for main meals, desserts and preserves and for lotions and potions. They have been hand-written by a number of people with varying levels of readability, grammatical and semantic accuracy. Certain recipes have a specific attribution such as the recipe for cheesecake provided by a Mrs Gwen Lanford Hope. One recipe, Burgess's Curry, has been cut from a magazine. Some recipes have also been used as scrap paper for various purposes such as arithmetical problems.

Some recipes are incomplete and others are often vague or just confusing typical of an oral tradition with local and individual variations and where it is assumed you will be an experienced cook and know what is meant by a 'handful'. Measures have also changed along with tastes and so some licence has been taken in the preparation of the recipes for modern usage. For example a modern pint equals 20 fluid oz. whereas it used to equal 16 fluid oz. as is still the case in the United States.

I have included some of the medicinal and domestic recipes so as to allow a more representative coverage of the document. It is not really possible - or desirable - to recreate the medicinal recipes but it does show us how versatile our forebears were.

I have chosen to arrange the recipes under general headings such as 'Soups and Stews'. There does not appear to have been any particular rationale for their presentation which meant that related items were scattered. Where there were two similar recipes I have made what I hope to be the choice of the more interesting one or included both if they have been of sufficient interest. The original recipes are reproduced to allow the enthusiastic to refer to them and are exactly as they were written, grammatical warts and all!

The collection reflects a home-grown culinary tradition in such recipes as Pease Soup Without Ham, Potted Beef and Hare Soup; in the use of caraway and oysters; and in the techniques used in the marmalade and damson cheese. Such recipes as that for orange or lemon cheesecake, in reality a curd spread, can be clearly traced back to 17th century cooks such as Hannah Glasse. The recipes were also reflecting more modern tastes with recipes such as that for Curry Powder though earlier recipes for curry can be found. The recipes also reflect the almost wanton abandon in the quantities used. The recipe for the Rich Cake requires 24 eggs while the Apple Jelly includes 27 lemons!!

The collection is not a copious or comprehensive one: there are no recipes, for example, for fish dishes while there are in comparison several recipes devoted to medicinal or domestic matters and quite wide coverage of puddings and condiments. This uneven coverage is probably due to the fact that the collection is the result of several individual inputs over a period of time and not the responsibility of one person. It is also highly probable, given the loose leaf nature of the documents, that some have been lost.

All that remains, therefore, is to wish you fun in recreating these dishes and enjoyment in the tasting of them.

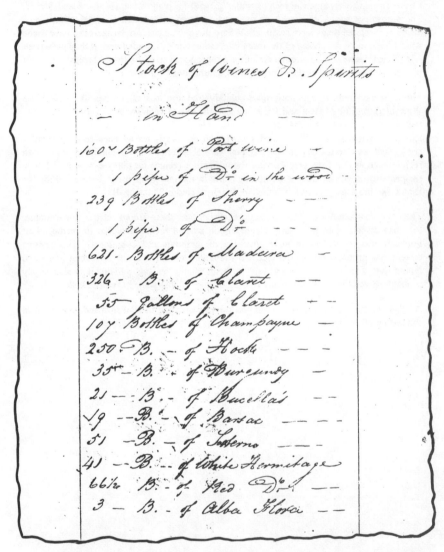

Stock of Wines & Spirits

in Hand

160 Bottles of Port wine
1 pipe of D° in the wood
239 Bottles of Sherry
1 pipe of D°
621 Bottles of Madeira
326 — B. of Claret
55 gallons of Claret
107 Bottles of Champagne
250 B. of Hock
35 B. of Burgundy
21 B. of Bucellas
19 B. of Barsac
51 B. of Sauterne
41 B. of White Hermitage
66½ B. of Red D°
3 B. of Alba Flora

A page from the inventory of contents, probably from the Hermitage, belonging to William Wilshere and dated 1824. It lists the wines and spirits, names and amounts, the latter amazing when one remembers that William lived alone, a widower since 1786.

SPRING SOUP
Serves 6

Making soups was an arduous job when starting with the making of the stock and finishing, where a smooth soup was required, with sieving the contents through a tammy, a large cloth requiring 2 people with 2 large wooden spoons. The liquidiser is truly a wonderful invention!

---

take 6 Carrots 4 heads of Celery 8 large Onions Slice all very thin and put into a Stewpan with a Small bit of Butter add a Small handful of parsley and a little thyme Draw it all down and then fill it up with pale Stock when done add a handful of spinach to give it a green colour and palp it through it through a tammy have a few asparagus tops Boiled and a Cucumber cut and fryed and put in when the soup is set to table season it to the palate

---

3 carrots
2 heads celery
3 large onions
1 pint (570 ml) chicken stock or two stock cubes
Small piece butter
Small handful parsley
Pinch thyme
Handful fresh or frozen spinach
10 asparagus tips or fried cucumber sticks

Slice the vegetables very thinly and place in a pan with a small piece of butter, a small handful of parsley and a little thyme. Cook gently over a medium heat and then add enough chicken stock to cover. Simmer gently until nearly done, season to taste and then add a handful of cooked spinach to give colour. To serve add a few cooked asparagus tips or a few sticks of fried cucumber.

PEASE SOUP WITHOUT HAM
Serves 6

Mrs Beeton, who describes her version as 'inexpensive' and 'Seasonable in winter', also omits meat though does use meat stock to enrich the soup. Francatelli, however, in his book for the working classes does include meat, whatever is available, and like Mrs Beeton includes a garnish of mint.

———————————

One dozen of large onions, cut them in slices add to them a handful of Celery, Lettuce or endive fry them brown, & put to them a pint of spilt pease, then pour on them a gallon of boiling water salt & spice to yr. taste, boil it till reduced to two quarts then pulp it thro a sieve before you send it to table have ready a little stewed spinach & celery to put in the tureen

———————————

6 large onions, sliced
Handful each of celery and lettuce or endive
8 oz (225 g) split peas
2 pints (1.2 litres) water
Salt and a small pinch of mace
Butter
Cooked spinach and celery for garnish

Fry the onions, celery and lettuce or endive in the butter until softened. Add the split peas, the water, salt and mace. Cook till the split peas are soft and the soup reduced by about a half and then liquidize or sieve if a smooth soup is required or leave if a more chunky texture is preferred. You may also prefer at this stage to add more liquid if the soup is too thick. Serve with the vegetable garnish.

MOLICATONY SOUP
Serves 6

Despite the description of this as a soup it is rather more substantial, more of a stew, and obviously intended to be accompanied by rice. It is rather better known as Mulligatawny soup, originally meaning 'pepper water' possibly from the Tamil 'milagu-tannir', and was for many decades a popular and persistent item on menus. Mrs Beeton includes a recipe for it using the more popular name. Her version too would make a substantial meal. She also includes a vegetable version though maintains that *'Nice pieces of meat...are necessary to make this soup good.'*

Take a couple of Chickens cut them up & blanch them, wash them in cold water trim them & cut them in small peices then take a pint of good veal or Beef stock put the drum sticks and necks of the Chickens into it with half a table spoonful of Curry Powder & let it boil about half an hour, add a quart more stock take 6 onions cut them in slices and fry them brown in a quarter of a pound of frish Butter put them into the stock & let them boil half an hour longer rub the whole thro' a seive or tammy take out the Bones & make the soup of a proper thickness then put the chicken in & let them boil till tender season with pepper & salt a little Cayon & Lemon juice serve it up in a Turren, Boil rice to eat with it. NB Rabbit will do if you have not Chicken veal broth if you have not Beef Stock

---

2lb (900g) chicken pieces
1½ pints (850 ml) chicken/veal stock
Half tblsp curry powder
3 onions finely chopped
2oz (50 g) butter
Lemon juice and seasoning

Wash, trim and brown the chicken in 1oz (25gm) of the butter and the curry powder. Add half the stock and simmer for about 30 minutes. Add the remaining stock and onions, fried in the remaining butter and cook for a further 30 minutes. Remove the meat, bone it and then return this to the pan. Reheat and season including the lemon juice. Serve with rice.

HARICO SOUP
Serves 6

Despite its name this dish does not include haricot beans. I initially assumed they must be an ingredient which for some strange reason had been omitted. The term 'harico', however, refers to a ragout. According to the Oxford English Dictionary it was first used in the 13th century related to the old French 'hericoq' and 'hericot' probably derived from 'harigoter' meaning 'to cut up'. Examples can be found in 18th century family receipt books such as Margaretta Acworth's collection where it is called 'herricoe' and in Mrs Rundell's 'Domestic Cookery' which includes ketchup as a flavouring.

Get a large neck of mutton cut it in two parts put the Scrag into a stew pan with four large turnips & four carrots in a Gallon of water let it Boil gently over a slow fire till all the goodness is out of the meat but not boiled to peices then bruise the Turnips & two of the carrots fine into the soup by way of thickening it cut & fry six onions in nice butter and put them then cut the other part of the mutton in small chops fry them in good butter and put them to the soup & let it stew very slowly till the chops are very tender. cut the other two carrots that were boild & put them in just before you take it off the fire & season it to your taste with pepper & salt & serve it up in a Tureen

---

12 lamb cutlets
8oz (225 g) stewing lamb
4 large turnips
4 carrots
6 onions
Butter or oil for frying
Flour

Place the stewing lamb, the turnips and two carrots in a pan, cover with water and stew gently for an hour. Leave to cool slightly, skim the fat off then strain off the stock. Beat the cutlets to tenderise the meat then dip them in flour and fry till lightly browned. Place the lamb in a stew pan add the remaining chopped vegetables and the stock. Cook gently on top of the cooker until the meat is tender, about 40 minutes. Serve with creamed potatoes.

HARE SOUP
Serves 6

The following made a very substantial 'soup' which I found went well with dumplings for those who enjoy a hearty meal. Mrs Beeton's version cooks all the meats together rather than roasting the hare. Phyllis Bentley's version of 1895, however, makes use of the leftover hare, probably roasted, and furthermore suggests using a gravy thickening if the soup is a little thin. I found a glass of red wine added a touch of richness.

Roast a Hare as if for table stuffed & when done & cold cut it in slices, put it in a Stewpan with two quarts of water & a 1/4lb. of Lean Bacon and a very small piece Lean Beef a bundle of sweet herbs and an onion or two when done strain it off take 2oz. of fresh Butter & brown it with flour in the stew pan. Then add the soup & a Glass of port wine with Cayenne according to your taste. NB the Beef may be wholly omitted & the soup will be just as good

---

1lb (450 g) cooked or uncooked hare cut into medium size pieces.
¼lb (110 g) lean bacon
¼lb (110 g) lean stewing beef
2 onions
Bundle of fresh sweet herbs such as thyme, marjoram and rosemary or 1 tsp. dried mixed herbs
2oz (50 g) butter
1oz (25 g) flour
Cayenne
Glass of red wine

Place the uncooked hare if used, the bacon, the beef, the onions and the herbs in a stewing pan and cover with water or beef stock. Simmer for a couple of hours adding the cooked hare, if used, for the last 30 minutes. Strain off the stock and reserve the meat. In another pan melt the butter and add the flour cooking for a minute or two. Gradually add enough stock and wine to make a sauce of the consistency of single cream. Return the meats to the pan and season with salt and cayenne.

POVEROY SAUCE

Maggie Black, the food historian, includes a similar recipe in her book described in the original as a *'Sauce for three boyld chickens'*. Both recipes produce a somewhat lumpy sauce but this can easily be sieved or blended to obtain a smoother version if this is preferred.

To Make poveroy Sauce take the yolk of an egg Boild Hard Brake it in a Bacon with a Spoon - With two tablespoonfulls of Sallad oil a Tea Spoonfull of maid mustard. Mixt well to Gather 3 anChovies 6 or 7 Eshalots a tablespoonfull of Capers all Chopt small & mixt With a little pepir salt & venigar to your tast a little parsley Chopt fine

----

1 egg, hard-boiled
2 tblsp salad oil
1 tsp made mustard, French
3 anchovies
6 shallots
1 tblsp capers
Seasoning and chopped parsley
White wine vinegar.

Mash the yolk with the oil and mustard. Pound together the anchovies, finely chopped shallots and chopped capers. Mix everything together, season with salt, pepper and enough vinegar to produce the desired consistency and decorate with the parsley.

OYSTER SAUCE

The redoubtable Phyllis Browne has 2 versions of this, the first using fresh oysters, the second making use of the tinned variety very useful these days when access to fresh oysters is not so easy or cheap. Her instructions for the latter sauce have formed the basis of this recipe. Either way the sauce is recommended as an accompaniment to mutton, perhaps a leg of lamb today.

Scald your oysters adding a little mace put in an anchovy or two if small with yr butter with a little flour then mix them together with as much of the liquid as will season them to yr taste & give them a boil up

---

1 pint oysters, cleaned, or a small tin of oysters.
Pinch of mace and nutmeg
2oz (50g) butter
1oz (25g) flour
1 pint (570ml) milk
Seasoning

If using fresh oysters scald them and place in a warm oven in a covered dish. Reserve the liquid. Make a roux from the flour and butter and add the oyster liquid, milk, spices and seasoning and cook for a minute. If the sauce is too thick add some more milk to make it the consistency of cream. If using tinned oysters use a little of the liquid they are preserved in. Add the oysters and heat through gently.

QUINS SAUCE

Mrs Beeton incudes a very similar recipe bearing the same name. The major difference appears to be the use of port wine - half a pint! - and a quarter of a pint of soy sauce which produces a more liquid item which is actually bottled. Recommended usage is with fish. I found that the following sauce went very well with cold salmon. The Wilshere recipe produces a more chunky sauce which you could liquidize if a smoother product is preferred. If you cannot get pickled mushrooms I suggest using mushroom ketchup or pickling your own! Mrs Beeton has a recipe.

Walnut pickle half a pint mushroom pickle half a pint 6 anchovies pounded 6 Cloves of Garlic sliced & bruised a teaspoonful of Cayenne pepper.

---

1 pint (570 ml) pickled walnuts
½ pint (275 ml) mushroom pickle or ¼ pint (150 ml) of mushroom ketchup
6 anchovies
6 cloves of garlic
2 tblsp red wine vinegar
Generous pinch of cayenne pepper

Mash the walnuts, mushrooms and anchovies using a pestle and mortar. Crush the garlic and add to the walnut mixture with a little cayenne. Add a little red wine vinegar to moisten the mixture. If desired liquidize the mixture. Adjust the consistency of the sauce if it is too thick by adding a little more vinegar.

GRAVY WITHOUT MEAT

Mrs Rundell's meatless gravy is also a spicy affair making use of small beer, walnut pickle and lemon peel amongst other ingredients. I found the following went well with sausages and grilled lamb chops.

Take five onions sliced, flour & fry them put them into a stew pan with a Quart of water let it simmer half a way a little Cayenne & Black pepper one lump of sugar a little salt two spoonfuls of Catchup one of Anchovy & thicken it with a little flour & butter.

---

3 onions
2oz (50 g) flour
2oz (50 g) butter
Small pinch of cayenne & black pepper
2 tblsp tomato ketchup
2 tblsp anchovy ketchup
Small lump of sugar
1 pint (570 ml) water or stock

Slice the onions, flour and fry them in butter. Gradually add the liquid and simmer till cooked. Add the remaining ingredients and cook for a further 5 minutes. If a smooth sauce is preferred liquidize the mixture adding more liquid if too thick.

BREAD SAUCE

Mrs Rundell includes a similar recipe in her Domestic Cookery but uses butter to enrich it rather than cream. Neither use nutmeg, a popular flavouring of mine for this sauce.

Slice some onion boil it in some milk & water with a little salt & whole pepper tender enough to beat up. Then pour it on a large piece of crumb of bread cover it up close & let it stand some time, then beat it well with a little cream & give it a boil up before it comes to table.

---

2 onions, sliced
1 pint (570 ml) milk and water
Salt and pepper
8oz (225 g) bread crumbs
2fl oz (55 ml) single cream

Cook the onions in the liquid with the seasonings till soft. Stir in the bread crumbs and leave to stand for an hour then cook over a low heat for about 10 minutes. If a softer sauce is required just use less bread crumbs. If a very smooth sauce is required briefly liquidize the mixture.

SAUCES

CURRY POWDER

By the time Phyllis Browne was writing purchasing prepared curry powders and pastes was perfectly acceptable. Mrs Beeton included a recipe based on Dr Kitchener's concoction along with various Indian 'chetneys'. In the footnote, however, she says:

'We have given this recipe for curry powder as some persons prefer to make it at home; but that purchased at any respectable shop is, generally speaking, far superior, and, taking all things into consideration, very frequently more economical.'

I would also add easier!! This recipe does, however, make a very good powder which seems to keep well.

To 3ozs of Coriander seed add 5ozs of Black pepper 3ozs Fenugreek 3ozs of Cummen seed & 6ozs of pale colourd Tamerick pound all these very fine then set them in a Dutch Oven before the fire to dry them well & keep turning them often when cold put them in a dry glafs bottle & keep them in a dry place they will keep 3 years This is tried & makes a very good Curry.

The ingredients for the Curry to be got from Mr.Godfrey's Southampton Street to be put in separate papers.

1½oz (40g) coriander seed.
2½oz (60g) black pepper
1½oz (40g) fenugreek
1½oz (40g) cumin seed
3oz (75 g) tumeric

Pre-heat the oven to Mark 3, 325°F or 170°C

Pound or preferably grind the spices till fine then place in the oven for about 1 hour to dry, turning the mixture frequently. When cooled bottle.

BURGESS'S CURRY
Serves 6

This recipe had been torn from a magazine. I have made it using the Wilshere curry powder recipe but any good prepared mild curry powder would do. The original is reproduced on the adjoining page.

---

1 medium chicken, jointed or a 3lb (1.35kg) bag of frozen chicken pieces.
Water or chicken stock
4oz (110g) butter
Medium onion
1 garlic clove
1 to 2 tblsp.curry powder (see curry powder recipe)
Salt & pepper

Place the chicken in a pan, cover with water or stock, add a dessertspoon of salt and simmer for about 45 minutes or until nearly cooked, skimming when necessary. In another pan lightly brown the butter and add the garlic, onion and curry powder and cook for 5 minutes. Add the chicken, reserving the stock, and brown. Add enough stock to form a good gravy and simmer for a further 30 minutes. Serve with plain boiled rice.

No. 107, *Corner of Savoy-Steps, Strand.*

B U R G E S S's

RECEIPT FOR MAKING A DISH OF CURRY,

AFTER THE INDIAN MANNER.

CUT two chickens as for fricasees, wash them clean, and put them in a stew-pan, with as much water as will cover them, sprinkle them with a large spoonful of salt, and let them boil till tender, covered close all the time, and skim them well; when boiled enough, take up the chickens, and put the liquor of them into a pan, then put half a pound of fresh butter in the pan, and brown it a little; put into it two cloves of garlick, and a large onion sliced; let these all fry till brown, often shaking the pan; then put in the chickens, and sprinkle over them two or three spoonfuls of Curry Powder; then cover the pan close, and let the chickens do till brown, often shaking the pan; then put in the liquor the chickens were boiled in, and let all stew till tender; if acid is agreeable, squeeze the juice of a lemon or orange in it.

DISH of RICE *to be served up, with the* CURRY *in a Dish by itself.*

Take half a pound of rice, wash it clean in salt and water, then put into it two quarts of boiling water, and boil it briskly for 20 minutes, then strain it in a cullender, and shake it into a dish, but do not touch it with your fingers, nor with a spoon.

N. B. Beef, veal, mutton, rabbits, fish, &c. may be curried and sent to table with or without the dish of rice.

The above Curry Powder is not only used in dishes that are curried, but is now used, and strongly recommended by the most approved Cooks in the kingdom, as a fine flavoured seasoning for fish, fowls, steaks, chops, veal-cutlets, hashes, minces, alamodes, turtle-soups, and in all rich dishes, gravies, sauce, &c. &c. and is equally cheap as common pepper, owing to its great strength.

It is also recommended by the most eminent Physicians, to be the most wholesome seasoning for all kinds of vegetables, particularly pease, beans, cucumbers, &c. &c. as it always keeps the stomach free from all windy complaints.

The recipe for Burgess's Curry

TAKE 6 CARROTS, 4 HEADS OF CELERY, 8 LARGE ONIONS ...

FRENCH BEEF STEAK
Serves 6

Mrs Beeton and Mrs Rundell both have recipes for 'Beef a la Mode' which is very similar to the following dish. The main differences seem to be the use of vinegar and port which would add a richness to the gravy. The original does suggest using rib but you could use sirloin or brisket. The original recipe title describes the dish as 'a good top Dish' a 'Dish for a small dinner and a remove for Fish', in other words an alternative meal, and also contains an interesting postscript regarding instructions to the cook.

Take one Rib of good fat Beef take out the Bone & Dobe the lean part with Bacon in ten or twelve places, roll it up quite tight, and skewer it thro' two ways to prevent its rising, tie it round with pack thread and fry it of a light brown put it into a stew pan, that will little more than hold it, fill the stew pan three parts with water, put in a little Whole Pepper, Allspice and salt to the taste, a bundle of sweet Herbs, Turnips, Carrots & Celery, let it stew four or five hours take out the Beef, & strain the Gravy skim off the fat, thicken your Gravy with flower, & Butter to the thickness of good Cream, season it to your taste, put in the Beef to keep it hot have ready boiled, some Button Onions, take up the Beef, & put in the Onions to the Gravy, take the strings & skewers from the Beef. leave the small end lose from the other put the Onions into the Dish and the Gravy over it, send it to Table quite hot.

4lb (2.25kg) beef, rib boned
10-12 rashers of streaky bacon
Whole black pepper and salt
Ground allspice
Bundle of fresh parsley, chives, thyme, savory, marjoram.
1 large turnip
3-4 carrots
1 head of celery
Beurre maniér made with 3 tblsp each of flour and butter
8oz (225g) boiled button onions
3oz (75g) butter

48

Finely chop half the herbs and spread over the meat. Carefully roll up the joint so the herbs are inside and skewer it to hold in place. Cover with the bacon slices then tie it tightly with string removing the skewers when this has been done. Place the joint in a close fitting pan and brown it in the butter. Add enough water or beef stock to cover the meat, a few whole black peppercorns and some salt. Cook slowly on top of the stove for about 3 hours then add vegetables, cut into medium size pieces, and cook for a further hour or so. Remove the beef and strain the gravy. Thicken it with the flour paste till it is the consistency of single cream. Serve the beef in a dish with the sauce and decorated with the boiled onions.

BLACK PUDDING

Home curing was a normal cooking activity up until the early years of this century and recipes such as this were common in recipe collections. Francatelli and Phyllis Browne both have recipes for sausages and Francatelli includes one for black pudding. The following is included, however, for academic interest though there may be a butcher willing to accept the challenge. The use of mace and pennyroyal, a type of mint, would probably make the sausage rather sweeter than the one we would recognise on a breakfast plate. As for the size of a twopenny loaf I can only recommend you to read the chapter on loaf weights in Elizabeth David's history of English bread and baking.

To a quart of large oatmeal put about a quart of hog's blood to steep the night before the puddings are to be made, pour a quart of boiling milk upon the crumb of a twopenny loaf sliced, four or five Eggs, some beaten mace, cloves, pepper, & salt, & a little pennyroyal, mix the oatmeal up the next morning with the bread, milk, Eggs, an spice. then melt half pound of Pork suet, strain the clean into the ingredients, put some cut pork suet as you like to have them for fatnefs, the ropes to be scraped very clean cut into proper lengths not to be more than half filled, then to be wash in cold water, & boild in a large quantity of water about ten minutes, then to be taken out & laid on some very clean straw & pricked with a pin, let them lye a few minutes & put them in to boil again about quarter an hour longer, then laid on straw again & very well rinfed. when cold taken off the straw, or a large hair sieve will do as well

---

A period advertisement for a local butcher

TO POTT BEEF

Potting has long been a popular way of preserving meat and a useful way of dealing with leftovers. Most collections have at least one recipe. Some use saltpetre as a preservative. This one uses 'salt prunella' about which I have found nothing assuming it to be a type of saltpetre. Unfortunately saltpetre is not easily available though a good butcher may be willing to supply it. As, however, it only serves to add colour to the meat and does not apparently affect its taste or keeping qualities it is not really a vital ingredient.

Take two or three pounds of lean Beef salt it with Common Salt and a little Salt Prunella, let it lay 3 or 4 days take it out of the brine put in a deep coarse pot, just cover it with water put a small bit of butter on the top; tie it down with brown paper, when properly Baket; wile hot take out of the liquor into a mortar pick of any fat or skin that may be in it; pound it well with a little of the liquor it was bake in and a little butter made hot; add a little pepper nutmeg mace and a very little cloves: put it down close into Pottery Pots and pour over clarifyd butter.

3lbs (1.35kg) brisket, boned but not rolled
3oz (75g) salt
1tsp saltpetre if available
6oz (175g) butter
Generous pinch of nutmeg and mace
Small pinch of cloves
Pepper
6oz (175g) clarified butter

Oven temperature Mark 3, 325°F or 170°C.

Rub the salt and saltpetre into the meat, place in a deep dish, cover with a cloth and leave in the fridge for 3 to 4 days turning twice a day. Rinse off the excess salt and soak in cold water for 2 hours. Place in a close fitting casserole and add a little water, 3oz (75g) of butter and the spices. Cover with foil and bake for 3 to 4 hours. Remove and while still warm cut out any fat or gristle. Then mash or pound the meat as finely as possible adding some seasoning and 3oz (75g) butter. Place in a dish and cover with clarified butter.

RICE PIE
Serves 6

Mrs Rundell has a similar recipe described as a '*Casserol, or Rice Edging, for a Currie, or Fricassee.*' The rice certainly makes a good surround for a hash using leftover meat and vegetables.

---

for A Rice pye Take a pd of Rice let it boil in good broth till the rice is tender then strain it from the broth & when cold put to it the yolk of an egg Mix it together with a little suet & form it into a case for a pye put a fricafsee into it & cover it with the same paste (if you chuse a top) glaze it with the yolk of an Egg to colour it in the oven you must bake something in it to keep its shape, a potery pan will do.

1lb (450g) rice, well rinsed
2 pints (1.2litres) veal or chicken stock
3 egg yolks
2oz (50g) suet

Pre-heat the oven to Mark 4, 350°F or 180°C

Cook the rice in the stock until tender. Strain and leave until cold. Add 2 egg yolks and the suet to the rice and mix. Use to line a dish about 2ins deep reserving some for a topping if desired. Brush with the last beaten egg yolk and bake in the oven until lightly browned. Do not allow to become too dry. Fill the rice case with a fricassee of your choice and if adding the topping glaze this with the third egg yolk and return to the oven for a further 10 to 15 minutes.

RICE PIE - A SECOND VERSION
Serves 6

This provides a slightly richer alternative to the previous recipe achieved through minor additions and alterations.

For the same Boil a pd of Rice in a quart of milk till it comes to a paste add a piece of Butter and some salt & a onion shape it with something in the middle to keep it hollow egg it over & put it in the oven or before the fire in the Dutch oven till it becomes a light brown then put in a fricassee of veal or Chicken

---

1lb (450g) rice, well rinsed
2 pints (1.2 litres) milk
2oz (50 g) butter
Salt and pepper
Finely chopped onion
Egg yolk

Pre-heat the oven to Mark 4, 350°F or 180°C

Boil the rice in the milk till tender and the add the butter, salt and onion. Use to line a dish, glaze with the egg and bake till light brown. Fill with a fricassee or hash of your choice.

SAVOURY RICE
Serves 4

Phyllis Browne has a version that is rather like a savoury rice pudding which she rather curiously serves with bubble and squeak. I would suggest serving this with sausages or grilled meat or on its own with a salad for a light supper dish.

Put a pound of rice into three quarters of boiling water skim the water then add an ounce of hog's fat beef or mutton suet cut into small thin strips let it continue boiling twenty minutes then add a little allspice and salt. set the pot by the side of the fire, close covered, so as barely to simmer for an hour and a quarter, when it will be fit for use. It will produce about eight pounds of drefsed rice. In an earthen pan, covered up, it will keep two or three days if it has been set by and is again to be prepared for eating, it should be gradualy warmed and stirred, if a morsel of Cheshire Cheese be grated into it it will greatly improve its flavour

---

8oz (225g) of rice, well rinsed
3 pints (1.7litres) of water or chicken stock
1oz (25g) lard or suet
½ tsp allspice
Salt
Grated Cheshire cheese to taste

Boil the rice in the water or stock, skim and add the lard or suet. Add the allspice and salt and simmer till cooked. Drain and serve with grated cheese which improves the flavour.

CHEESE PUDDING
Serves 3

This makes a surprisingly tasty and rich meal, good hot or cold, which would go well with a mixed salad. It would be interesting to experiment with the addition of some smoked ham to the pudding or perhaps a layer of tomatoes. It is interesting that Gloucester or Cheshire are recommended. In Mrs Beeton's book Cheshire cheese receives high praise apparently *'famed all over Europe for its rich quality and fine piquant flavour.'* It is of further interest, too, that she talks about the possibilities of colour adulteration and that it was not unknown for the dye annatto to contain red lead!

Three eggs very well beat, half a pound of good Gloucester or Cheshire Cheese grated; a little salt & nutmeg to your taste, take a Gill of good cream The dish must be buttered & in a Quick Oven. Ten minutes will bake it, the whites of the eggs are used

---

3 eggs, beaten
8oz (225g) Gloucester or Cheshire cheese, grated
Salt and nutmeg
5 fl oz (150ml) single cream

Pre-heat the oven to Mark 5, 375°F or 190°C

Mix all the ingredients together thoroughly. Pour into a greased dish and bake in the oven for about 25 minutes. You may prefer to grate the nutmeg on the top as for a custard.

TOASTED CHEESE
Serves 2 to 3

Cheese was not always so highly regarded as a food, thought rather dull and not easily digested. Gordon Grimley in his collection of Victorian recipes, however, has included a rather grand royal version which uses champagne and ale, this mixed with the cheese which is then melted and served with toast. The following example, though rather more plebeian, is, however, quite delicious. A salamander in this case was not a lizard but a circular iron plate which was heated and then placed over the item to brown it.

---

six ounces of cheese two ditto butter the yolk of one egg beat to a paste in a mortar Then spread it on some round pieces of bread toasted on one side, brown them with a salamander & send them to table

---

6oz (175g) grated mature cheddar or other hard English cheese,
2oz (50g) butter
Egg yolk
2-3 slices of bread toasted on one side

Beat the cheese, butter and egg together. Spread the mixture evenly on the untoasted side of bread and grill till lightly browned.

STEWED PEAS
Serves 6

Mrs Rundell's recipe recommends the use of *'a good piece of butter'* or beef or pork, salted if desired. The latter would obviously make a richer dish. Note that the amount of sugar referred to is a lump indicating that this would have been a sugar cone they were using.

Fry some old peas in butter, put them in a little water to stew, till they are tender with a bunch of sweet herbs, some chives, & a shank of ham. They must stew about two hours, when they are almost enough, put in a pretty large lump of sugar, a few slices of ham to send up with them

---

8oz (225g) dried peas
2lb (900g) ham, soaked to remove the excess salt
2oz (50g) butter
Sweet herbs such as thyme and marjoram
Tablespoon of sugar

Fry the peas in the butter then add the ham, herbs and enough water to cover them. Cook gently for about 2 hours. Add the sugar towards the end. Serve with root vegetables.

POTATOE PUDDING
Serves 6

The potato was often used as an ingredient in sweet items. The Receipt Book of Mrs Ann Blencowe 1694 has a rich recipe - one pound of butter to one pound of potatoes - for a potato pudding to be served as a dessert item while Mrs De Salis in 1888 has a recipe for potato cheesecakes where the filling is baked in a pastry shell. I like this pudding very much and would also suggest the inclusion of a handful of sultanas and some spice, perhaps nutmeg.

6oz potatoes boiled and pounded 3oz butter 3oz sugar 1 egg & the juice of one lemon & the peel boiled and pounded & then baked

---

6oz (175g) boiled potatoes
3oz (75g) butter
3oz (75g) sugar, perhaps a mixture of white and brown
1 egg
Juice and grated peel of one lemon

Pre-heat the oven to Mark 4, 350°F or 180°C

Mash the potato thoroughly and then mix with the remaining ingredients. Place in a greased dish and bake for about 30 minutes until browned.

HUNTERS PUDDING
Serves 6

This is really another version of Christmas Pudding though containing more bread crumbs and suet than we are used to. Mrs Beeton's version, also called Hunter's Pudding, uses more fruit and will make a moister and richer pudding than the Wilshere alternative. Mrs Rundell's recipe uses 6 *'Jamaica peppers in fine powder'* which I take to mean allspice. If you are unsure about the amount of suet then reduce this by 4oz (110g) and add this amount in bread crumbs to the mixture.

———————

one pd beef suet pd raisons six spoonfuls flour six Eggs two spoonfuls cream some nutmeg & sugar to your taste 2 spoonfuls Brandy boil it four or five hours.

———————

1lb (450g) beef or a vegetarian suet
1lb (450g) raisins
6 dsp of flour
6 large eggs, beaten
2 tblsp single cream
Nutmeg
6oz (175g) light soft brown sugar
2 tblsp brandy

Mince or finely chop the raisins then add to the other ingredients and mix together thoroughly. Place in a greased 2lb pudding bowl or in 2 smaller bowls and cover with a pleated and greased paper circle and a pleated piece of foil. Boil for about 4 hours.

VERMICELLI PUDDING
Serves 6

Phyllis Browne includes an almost identical recipe the only difference being that she bakes hers while the following recipe suggests cooking on the stove. I suspect most people would find baking the easier proposition. I did!

Boil a pint of milk with a little lemon peal and Cinnamon when boild a few minutes add about an ounce of vermicelli let it boil half an hour quietly; put a bit of Butter about the size of a walnut a little nutmeg and sugar to your tast 4 Eggs and boil it about an hour and half

---

1 pint (570ml) full cream milk
Piece of fresh lemon peel
½ tsp cinnamon
1oz (25g) pasta vermicelli
Walnut sized piece of butter
Nutmeg
1oz (25g) caster sugar
4 eggs, beaten

Pre-heat the oven to Mark 4, 350°F or 180°C

Bring the milk with the lemon peel and cinnamon to the boil. Remove the lemon peel. Add the vermicelli and gently cook for about 30 minutes. Add the butter, a little nutmeg, the sugar, beaten eggs and place in a greased baking dish. Place the dish in a baking tin containing hot water (bain-marie) and bake for about 45 minutes or until set.

Vermicelli Pudding

boil a pint of Milk with a little lemon peal and Cinnamon when boild a few minuits add about an ounce of vermicella let it boil half an hour gently; put a bit of Butter about the size of a walnut a little nutmeg and Sugar to your tast 4 Eggs and boil it about an hour and half

February 16 1824

The recipe for the Vermicelli Pudding, dated 1824

DERBYSHIRE PUDDING
Serves 6

Francatelli has two recipes for batter puddings, one making a thicker batter including your choice of fruits the other making a much lighter pudding, this recipe including precise instructions for baking in a tea cup. Mrs Beeton and Mrs Rundell also have examples, Mrs Rundell's instructions including the cooking together of the milk and flour prior to the addition of the other ingredients. Mrs Beeton also includes boiled and baked versions.

To a pint of milk add by degrees two table spoonfuls of flour & mix it very well with the milk and boil it till it is thick - Set it by till it is cold, then add a quarter of a pound of Butter melted, a quarter of a pound of fine Sugar a little salt the rind of a Lemon grated the yolks of 5 Eggs and the whites of 3 - put a paste round the edges of the pudding dish, and when the Pudding is baked put currant jelly on the top

1 pint (570ml) milk
2 tblsp flour
4oz (110g) unsalted butter
4oz (110g) caster sugar
Grated rind of 1 lemon
5 egg yolks, beaten
3 egg whites, beaten till quite stiff.
Pinch of salt
Redcurrant jelly

Pre-heat the oven to Mark 4, 350°F or 180°C

Make a paste with the flour and some of the milk, place in a saucepan and then carefully add the remaining milk. Bring slowly to the boil then lower the heat and cook until slightly thickened. Cool. Add the remaining ingredients, folding in the whites last of all. Place in a greased dish and bake for 45 minutes. Serve with redcurrant jelly.

SMALL BAKED PUDDINGS
Serves 4

This somewhat unprepossessing dish makes a very pleasant pudding best served warm and with a wine enriched custard. It may well be similar to the dish that John Wilshere was reputed to have much enjoyed.

———————————

a quarter of a pound of grated Bread 2 ounces of suet chopped fine half a pint of milk, three egg yolks, 2 whites sugar & nutmeg to your taste baked in cups half filled with wine sauce

———————————

4oz (110g) white bread crumbs
2oz (50g) suet
10fl.oz (275ml) full cream milk
3 egg yolks and 2 whites
2oz (50g) caster sugar
Nutmeg

Pre-heat the oven to Mark 4, 350°F or 180°C

Mix the bread crumbs, suet and sugar together. Beat the egg yolks and milk together thoroughly and stir into the bread mixture. Whip the whites till reasonably stiff but not too dry and carefully fold into the bread mixture. Place this in a greased dish and bake for about 30 minutes till set but still soft. Serve warm.

BAKED APPLE PUDDING
Serves 6

There are various similar recipes to be found in Mrs Beeton one of which is described as a cheesecake. I would suggest baking the apple mixture in a pastry case though this is by no means essential. Surprisingly none of the recipes use any spices. A 'runnet' I have taken to be a corruption of 'reinette' an apple with a good flavour and late keeping qualities

---

Peel & quarter eight Golden runnets or 12 Gold pippens Throw them into water in which boil them as for sauce sweeten them with loaf sugar squeeze in two lemons & grate the peels six Eggs well beat, beat all well together cover your dish with a thin paste & bake it an hour in a slow oven.

---

8 Coxes apples
2 lemons, juice and grated peel
2oz (50g) sugar
6 eggs, beaten
6oz (175g) shortcrust pastry

Pre-heat the oven to Mark 4, 350°F or 180°C

Peel and thinly slice the apples and cook them gently in a little water. Add the sugar, lemon juice and rind. Beat in the eggs and place in a baking dish lined with pastry. Bake for about 30 minutes or till the apple filling is set.

BAKED APPLE PUDDING (2)
Serves 6

This version makes a less rich dessert. Perhaps the use of spice is to compensate for this fact. I have used macaroons as a possible alternative to a Naples biscuit whose origin I have been unable to establish.

---

18 Golden pippens or 8 Golden Runnets peel & core them & beat them in a marble mortar take 4 Eggs the whites of 2 Nutmeg, Clove & sugar to your taste the juice of an orange or Lemon 2 spoonfuls of cream 2 Naples biscuits a piece of paste round the edge

---

9 Coxes apples
2 eggs
1 extra egg white.
Nutmeg and clove
2oz (50g) sugar
Juice of a small lemon and small orange.
1-2 tblsp of cream.
2oz (50g) macaroons, crushed

Pre-heat the oven to Mark 4, 350°F or 180°C

Cook the apples till soft. Mix in the remaining ingredients and place in a greased dish. Bake for about 40 minutes or till set.

TO STEW GOLDEN PIPPINS
Serves 6

Such desserts were popular as light conclusions to a luncheon or as Mrs Rundell says *'as an elegant and good dish for a corner'.*

---

18 Golden Pippens peel them & core them whole Throw them into water then take ¾ of a pd of fine sugar a pint & half of water & the white of one egg beat to a froth Stir it together & set it on a charcoal fire when it boils skim it well then put in the apples let them boil slow & when clear take them out squeeze a large Lemon or 2 small one into the syrup give it a boiling & pour it upon the pippens.

---

9 dessert apples
6oz (175g) sugar
¾ pint (425ml) water + extra for cooking apples
1-2 lemons squeezed

Peel and core the apples and cook them whole, carefully in a little water. Mix and cook the sugar and water and boil for about 5 minutes till syrupy. Add the apples and cook over a low heat for a further 10 minutes. Strain, placing the apples in a serving dish, and add the lemon juice to the syrup boiling for a further five minutes. Pour over the apples and chill.

CHEESECAKES
Serves 6

There are several variations on this theme. Some use the filling in a pastry case and some fillings more closely resemble what we would call lemon curd. Mrs Rundell has a similar recipe to the following though she uses curd cheese as in a modern cooked cheesecake. This recipe does, however, make a very delicious dessert described in the original as a '*good one*' provided courtesy of a Mrs Gwen Lanford Hope.

---

a quarter of a pint of cream boild. 5 yolks of Eggs half the whites beat them very well Take the cream off the fire & pour in the Eggs carefully that it does not curdle, set it over the fire & keep it stirring like it is a thick curd. When cold add 2 or 3 ounces of melted Butter, sugar to your taste. grate in some nutmeg, beat one ounce of sweet almonds in a little basin or orange flower water (not too small) & put in your Cheesecakes & 2 ounces of Currants washed clean. Don't fill your pans too full or let them stand long in the pans before they go into the Oven - if they do they are likely to be heavy. You may add sweetmeat cut in if you like it - or grate in a little lemon peel

---

5 fl oz (150ml) double cream
5 egg yolks, beaten and 2-3 egg whites, beaten till they hold their shape
2-3oz (50-75g) unsalted butter, melted
1oz (25g) caster sugar
1oz (25g) ground almonds
1 tblsp orange flower or rose water
2oz (50g) currants
Nutmeg

Pre-heat the oven to Mark 4, 350°F or 180°C.

Heat the cream to nearly boiling point. Remove from the heat and pour onto the egg yolks mixing thoroughly. Return to a low heat and stir constantly till slightly thickened. When cooled add the remaining ingredients folding in the egg whites. Fill greased individual ramekin dishes or a single large one. Place in a baking tin half full of hot water and bake for about 20 minutes for the small versions and 40 minutes for a large pudding.

DUTCH FLUMMERY
Serves 4

Mrs Rundell has a Dutch Flummery recipe which uses isinglass to help set the mixture. The ingredients are also cooked briefly, 'scalded' in the original, so that one ends up with a rich wine egg custard cum jelly. Isinglass was used as a clarifying and adhesive substance and for preserving eggs.

---

put to an oz. of Isinglafs a pint of boiling water the rind of a Large Lemon grated let it stand covered till quite cold then add the juice of two lemons & the yolks of four Eggs well beat & two cups of White Wine mix all together

---

4 egg yolks, well beaten
2 lemons
2oz (50g) caster sugar
2 cups of white wine
1 pint (570ml) boiling water
1 sachet of gelatine.

Mix together the sugar, water and the rind of one lemon. When the syrup has cooled add the juice of both lemons, the egg yolks and wine and beat well over hot water till slightly thickened. Dissolve the gelatine according to the instructions on the sachet and add to the mixture. Pour into a serving dish and leave to set. Serve chilled with a flavoured cream and decorated if desired.

ITALIAN CHEESE
Serves 6

The following is a type of syllabub and is simplicity itself. Mrs Rundell has a similar recipe for a strained cream dish made richer by the inclusion of a sweet wine which she suggests serving with biscuits made from puff pastry with sugared tops.

———————

one gl of Cream the peel of a large Lemon grated the juice of 3 sweeten to your taste whisk it up & as the froth rises pretty thick take it off put in a sieve with a fine piece of Muslin for it to drain thro' raise the sieve on sticks over a dish let it stand 5 or so hours then put a dish over it & turn it up take off the sieve gently & the muslin. The size of the sieve should be six inches deep & over.

———————

2 pints (1.2 litres) double cream
Juice of 2 large lemons and the grated peel of one.
4oz (110g) icing sugar

Whisk all the ingredients together making sure not to beat the cream too stiffly. Serve in a large bowl or in individual dishes decorated as wished.

GINGER BISCUITS

The following recipe was tagged on to the recipe for Lemon Jam. The original contained the ingredient 'jalap' which was obtained from a tropical plant and used as a purgative. I assume that the original biscuit was, therefore, intended for medicinal rather than pleasurable purposes. I have omitted this item but found that the remaining ingredients make a spicy biscuit for those ginger lovers.

1pd. of flour, 1pd. treacle, three oz. of loaf sugar, 3oz Butter, ½ an oz. of beaten Ginger, one oz & half of pounded jalap, mix the ingredients well together make them up in little cakes & bake them in a Slack oven.

1lb (450g) flour
1lb (450g) golden syrup and treacle mixture according to taste
3oz (75g) caster sugar
3oz (75g) butter, softened
1tsp or more if desired of ground ginger

Pre-heat the oven to Mark 4, 350°F or 180°C

Mix all the ingredients together very thoroughly to a soft dough. A food processor does this job very well. Leave to rest for a while in the fridge then roll out reasonably thinly and cut out rounds. Place on a greased tray and bake for about 10 minutes or until lightly browned. This will make at least 25 biscuits depending on the size.

SMALL TEACAKES (1)

Mrs Beeton's recipe is richer using double the quantities of sugar and butter and also using eggs. Mrs Rundell's version, called Water Cakes, makes use of hot milk to bind the ingredients. The Wilshere recipe tends to make a drier biscuit which I found goes well with cheese.

A Pound of flour, two ounces of butter, a tablespoonful of yeast, two ounces of sugar a few carriway seeds this will make sixty cakes rolled out thin

---

1lb (450g) flour
2oz (50g) butter
2oz (50g) caster sugar
2tsp caraway seeds
Milk to mix

Pre-heat the oven to Mark 4, 350°F or 180°C

Sift the flour, rub in the butter and then mix in the remaining dry ingredients. Add enough milk to bind together. Roll out thinly on a lightly floured surface and cut out rounds. Place on a lightly greased tray and bake for about 10 to 15 minutes. This should make about 60 biscuits depending on their size.

TEA CAKES (2)

This obviously will make a richer biscuit more like Mrs Beeton's though the concentration of caraway seed may not be to everyone's taste.

To three quarters of a pound of flour add half a pound of Butter & rub it into the flour, then put half a pd of sifted sugar & one ounce of Carraway Seeds, mix all these ingredients together with one Egg, Role them out in thin Cakes and bake them on a Tin if one Egg is not sufficient to make them of a proper stiffnefs put a little milk

---

12oz (350g) flour
8oz (225g) butter
8oz (225g) caster sugar
1oz (25g) caraway seeds
1 egg
Milk

Pre-heat the oven to Mark 4, 350°F or 180°C

Sift the flour and rub in the butter. Add the sifted sugar, caraway seeds, egg and milk if needed. Roll out thinly on a floured surface, cut out rounds, prick with a fork and bake till lightly browned.

RUSKS

The rusk conforms to the original meaning of biscuit being cooked twice and so may well be a descendant of the old ship's biscuit renowned for its hard and durable nature! The word 'rusk' is possibly derived from the 16th.century Spanish or Portuguese 'rosca' meaning 'screw' perhaps indicating a twisted bread. Like Beeton's and Rundell's recipes, however, the following makes a rich dough. Mrs Beeton suggests omitting the sugar if the biscuits are intended for use with cheese while Mrs Rundell feels that the inclusion of caraway seed is suitable if the biscuit is to be eaten cold. This recipe is also interesting for the relatively detailed instructions on keeping the dough warm, making use of a 'reflector', presumably a metal sheet, to be used along the lines of a Dutch Oven by being placed before the fire.

Take 2lb of flour, 2oz Loaf Sugar grated - 6oz of Butter rubbed in to the Flour - Beat up 4 eggs - 3 large spoonsful of quite new yeast put to the beaten Eggs - then pour it to the Flour and Butter - Then put ½ a Pint of new Milk hot, and work it up. - Make them into small Balls, and put them into a Tin & set them by a Fire, an hour and an half to rise, keeping the Air from them as much as possible by setting the Reflector before them.- They take ¼ Hour Baking - Then cut them through with a sharp Knife, and set them into the oven , when almost cold, to dry

---

2lb (900g) flour, sifted
2oz (50g) caster sugar, 1 tsp reserved if using fresh yeast
6oz (175g) butter
4 eggs
1oz (25g) fresh yeast or equivalent dried yeast
10fl oz (275ml) of warm milk

Pre-heat the oven to Mark 6, 400°F or 200°C

Rub the butter into the flour and add the sugar. Prepare the fresh yeast by creaming it together with the reserved sugar and half of the heated milk. Leave in a warm place till frothy. If you are using dried yeast follow the manufacturer's instructions. Add the beaten eggs, yeast mixture and the remaining milk to the dry ingredients and knead briefly. Leave to rise in the bowl covered with a damp tea towel until doubled in size. Knock back the dough and knead again briefly. Divide into 24 pieces or more if smaller rusks are preferred forming these into flat tea cake shapes. Place on a greased baking tray, cover with the damp tea towel and leave to rise. Bake for about 20 minutes then split in half and return to the oven for 5 to 10 minutes to dry out or longer if necessary but do not let them become rock hard. This dough also makes excellent plain rolls if preferred to the rusks.

An advertisement for a local baker keen to appeal to a wide audience

RUSKS (2)

The inclusion of the lemon rind makes this rusk a very pleasant contrast to the previous recipe. As with the previous recipe the dough can just be used to make bread rolls.

One pound of flour, quarter of a pound of Butter, sugar and Lemon Peel. a little warm milk, a large spoonful of yeast let it stand some time to rise, then roll it up into small pieces, some take them a quarter of an hour in tins when cold cut them in two and dry them in tins in the oven. The above quantity makes about 36 pieces.

1lb (450g) flour
4oz (110g) butter
2oz (50g) sugar
Lemon peel
10fl oz (275ml) warm milk
1oz (25g) fresh yeast or a sachet of dried yeast

If using fresh yeast prepare it by mixing it with a teaspoon of sugar and 5fl oz of the milk. Leave it in a warm place for 15 minutes. If using dried yeast follow the manufacturer's instructions. Sift the flour and rub in the butter. Add the sugar, lemon peel and yeast then mix in the milk. Knead briefly and leave to rise in a warm place. When about doubled in size knock back, knead and form into small tea cake shapes. Bake in a hot oven for about 20 minutes then take out, slice in two and return to the oven to for 5 to 10 minutes to dry out. Makes about 20 rusks depending on the size.

PLAIN BISCUITS

The following recipes, written on the same sheet, make two rather different biscuits. Both would have gone well with cheese. The first would have made a rather dry biscuit having no fat ingredient, the description of 'plain' being entirely apt. It would also have needed to be eaten fresh. The second biscuit is described as 'iced' presumably because sugar is one of the ingredients. Caraway is included, a flavouring much favoured by 18th and 19th century cooks though not so popular today. I have included both original recipes but only adapted the second as being the more appetising of the two.

For Plain Biscuits make warm new milk as warm as you can work it in the Flour make it into a paste rather stiff roll them about the thicknefs of a penny piece bake them in moderate oven as they require a little drying.

For Iced Biscuits to about a pound of flour Take a bit of butter the size of a Walnut rub your butter well into the flour and a few carraway seed then warm your milk with about the same Quantity of Butter and some moist sugar mix your past as before Roll them thinner and this require a Quicker oven than the Plain ones.

1lb (450g) flour
2oz (50g) butter
1 tsp caraway seeds
2oz (50g) caster sugar
Warm milk to mix

Pre-heat the oven to Mark 5, 375°F or 190°C

Rub the butter into the flour. Add the caraway seeds, sugar and enough milk to mix to a pliable dough. Roll out quite thinly and cut out rounds. Bake for about 10 minutes.

RICH CAKE

There is something mythical about the stories one hears of the vast amounts of ingredients cooks supposedly used in such items as cakes. The following recipe, however, gains support from the likes of Mrs Rundell whose recipe for a 'Very Fine Cake' is daunting not just because of the ingredients but because of the incredible amount of time and effort required to make it. She suggests beating the ingredients together '*a full hour at least*'. One pities the poor servants responsible for its production! The recipe makes use of sweetmeats which in this instance I have taken to mean candied peels and sack. Some confusion reigns over whether sack was a dry or sweet wine, the name possibly derived from 'sec' meaning dry. There is, however, more agreement that sack wines came from Spain, Portugal and the Canaries. Perhaps it was related to sherry in the manner of production. Confusion apart the following recipe obviously used a lot of it and as modern day compromise I suggest using a medium sweet sherry. A final point of interest is the amount of nutmeg used and the absence of other spices. One would expect the nutmeg flavouring to be overwhelming but the cooking process seems to mellow its effect.

To make a rich Cake

3 pd of Flower well dryd & sifted the same quantity of Butter well washed from the salt a pound & half of Loaf sugar dried & sifted 3 nutmegs a pound of sweetmeats a pound of sweet Almonds a pint of sack five pounds of currants & 24 eggs.

Make it thus

Work your Butter till almost a cream put in the flower work that well then the sugar then the Almonds spice sweetmeat & currants then the yolk of the eggs which must be well beat then the wine you must beat the whites of the eggs to a froth & as it rises put it into the cake two hours & half will bake it in a quick oven.

1½lb (700g) flour
1½lb (700g) butter
1½ nutmegs
12oz (350g) dark brown sugar
8oz (225g) mixed peel
8oz (225g) sweet almonds
½ pint (275ml) medium sweet sherry
2½lb (1.15kg) currants
12 eggs, separated

Pre-heat the oven to Mark 3, 325°F or 170°C

Cream the butter and work in the sugar, then add the beaten egg yolks followed by the almonds, spice, peel and currants. Add the flour alternatively with the wine to the above mixture .Beat the egg whites to a froth and fold in. Place in a prepared tin (9" square or round) and bake for about 4 hours. Cover the top with foil or paper if it seems to be browning too much.

BREAD

This and the following yeast recipe are included purely for interest's sake. To reproduce the bread recipe would require using the yeast mixture which is not practicable. Bread and brewing were for centuries related occupations the former dependant upon the yeast from brewing to make the bread, which is why the yeast is referred to as a liquid measure.

---

a peck of flour, take near ½ a pint of yeast beat one egg into the yeast mix with milk or milk & water & set by the fire for about ½ an hour to rise bout a handful of salt after it has risen then nead it well & let it stand an hour or there abouts, then make it into a loaf & 3 hours will take.

The recipe for French Bread which uses milk *'warm from the cow'*

YEAST

Compressed yeast, also called German Yeast and confusingly dried yeast, began to appear in England in the mid-nineteenth century. Until then ale and beer yeasts or yeasts obtained from a solution made from fermented items such as potatoes or grain were used. Such yeasts would have been by-products of home brewing. These yeasts, however, were unreliable, unstable and difficult to produce. Many household cookery collections did, however, contain a yeast recipe and Mrs Rundell had recipes for yeast which are similar to the following. Perhaps home brewers will be inspired to try the following!

Take a peck of mealy Potatoes roast them in an oven till soft so as to rub them thro' a hair sieve put to them as mush boiling water as will make them the consistency of common Beer yeast to every pound of Potatoes 2ozs of coarse brown sugar and 2 Large spoonfulls of good small beer yeast keep it warm till it has done fermenting and in twenty four hours it will be fit for use. A pound of Potatoes makes nearly a Quart of yeast it will keep a month in cool weather it takes a large quantity to make your Bread than the common yeast & it should be made over night or five or six hours before it is baked, it has this advantage over beer yeast your bread is never bitter & always a good colour.

APPLE JELLY

This recipe is fascinating for the number of lemons required - 27 in all! The resulting jelly is, however, very good, even with half the amount. Codlins were a variety of cooking apple and I assume that 'russelings' is a corruption of 'russet' though I have not been able to verify this.

A ¼ peck Russelings or Codlins peel & cut them in pieces put them a preserving pan cover them with water put the rind of 3 Lemons a bit of cinnamon & a few cloves tied in a bit of muslin boil it altogether put it thro a flannel bag to each pint of apple syrup put one pd of Loaf sugar the juice of 2 dozen Lemons boil it over a slow fire till it becomes a jelly put it in pots with Brandy paper over

---

4lb (1.80kg) cooking apples
Rinds of 2 lemons
Juice of 12 lemons
Cinnamon stick and 1 tsp cloves
Water
Granulated or preserving sugar

Cut the apples, place in a pan and cover with water. Place the lemon rind and the spices in a muslin bag. Place the bag in the apples and cook to a pulp. Strain through a jelly bag and to every pint of apple juice add a pound of sugar and all the lemon juice. Cook over a low heat till the sugar has melted and then boil till it sets. Pot as for jam.

FRUIT BISCUITS

This recipe dates back to a much earlier culinary tradition of preserving and sweetmeats that can be seen in the 16th. and 17th. centuries. In such recipes the fruit, traditionally quince or orange, was boiled to a very thick consistency, boxed up and left to dry sometimes in or near a warm oven. The result was then a rather concentrated and sweet 'cake' or sweetmeat. Obviously such confections were still popular in the nineteenth century. The storage instructions are also interesting suggesting that conditions could be damp and conducive to mould formation, not ideal at all.

After baking the fruit pulp it through a sieve and allow a pound of fruit a pound of Loaf sugar pounded & sifted and the white of one egg another must stand by with two table spoons & put in a spoonful of fruit & a spoonful of sugar till the whole is mixd with the egg it will take two hours perhaps more to beat up the whole to the proper state after which you must put it into paper & dry them carefully They do not dry so well in an oven.

These biscuits may be made of any fruit & they will keep a twelvemonth or longer if looked at occasionally and placed before a fire.

2lbs (900 g) fruit, e.g. apples
Granulated or preserving sugar

Pre-heat the oven to Mark 1, 275°F or 140°C

Cook the fruit in a little water and cook to a pulp. Weigh this and the equivalent amount of sugar. Beat these two together, adding the sugar gradually. This will take quite a long time. Put into a lined container and place in the oven to dry skimming the surface if it appears to be drying too quickly.

DAMSON CHEESE

As with the previous recipe for the fruit biscuits this preserve is another example of an old tradition, a fruit cheese being a solid jam capable of being turned out and sliced. Plenty of examples abound in old recipe collections.

---

3 pounds of stoned Damsons to one pound of moist sugar boil them to a proper consistency keeping them stirring all the time.

3lb (1.35 kg) damsons, stoned
1lb (450 g) sugar

Place the ingredients in a preserving pan and melt the sugar over a low heat. Once melted raise the heat and cook till set, traditionally when a wooden spoon leaves a definite impression. Bottle as for jam.

ORANGE MARMALADE

Again this makes a rather thick confection, more a sweetmeat than a preserve as we expect. Mrs Rundell has a similar recipe though does not prescribe Seville oranges hence her use of apple juice probably for its pectin content.

Cut in two the cleanest seville oringes take out all the pulp & juice in a bason pick all the skins & seeds out of it Boil the Rinds in hard water 2 or three times while they be Boiling - then pound them in a marble mortar add to it the juice & pulp put them in a preserving pan with Double its weight of Loaf sugar set it over a slow fire Boil it Rather more than halfe an hour put it in to pots Cover it with Brandy paper tie it Close Down.

---

2 Seville oranges
Sugar

Pare the rinds, cook in water till softened then liquidize using a little of the cooking liquid Squeeze the juice, mix with the rind pulp and then weigh. Place this in a preserving pan with double its weight in sugar. Cook over a gentle heat till the sugar has dissolved then raise the heat and stir until set. Pot as for jam.

ORANGE CHEESECAKE

The instructions for the following are minimal to say the least, very much in the verbal tradition where experience counted for everything. The result with a little amending produces a very good orange curd. Sweet oranges could be substituted and unsalted butter used.

Take the inside & juice of Nine seville oranges & grate the rind
of 2 an oz. of Butter clarifyd one egg sweeten it to your taste

---

9 Seville oranges
1oz (25g) butter
2 eggs, beaten
4oz (110 g) sugar

Grate the rinds of 2 oranges and squeeze the juice from all of them. Place these ingredients in a pan with the sugar and butter and place over a low heat until these last 2 ingredients are melted. Then add the eggs mixing thoroughly and cook over a low heat, stirring constantly until the mixture has thickened. Pot as for jam.

LEMON JAM

Mrs Rundell includes a similar recipe using Seville oranges with the addition of rose water. Her version was obviously intended to be served as a dessert.

Beat up six Eggs leaving out the whites of two, grate the rinds of two Lemons & take the juice of three, 1 pd Lump Sugar broken small ¼ pd of good fresh Butter, put the above ingredients into a Stew Pan over a slow fire stirring them all the time till they are dissolved & begin to thicken, put them into a jar & when cold tie it down & it will keep for several months.

---

6 egg yolks
4 whites beaten together
Grated rind of 2 lemons
Juice of 3 lemons
1lb (450 g) sugar
4oz (110 g) butter

Place all the ingredients in a pan and cook over a low heat stirring till the sugar has dissolved and the mixture thickened. Pot and cover when cold.

TO BOTTLE CURRANTS

Mrs Rundell's recipe suggests collecting the fruit making sure it is dry, placing these in a bottle which is then corked and covered in resin and then placed in a trench in the garden. No mention is made of any cooking process. Ruth Mott, in the Victorian Kitchen, describes a more familiar process of bottling red currants though the fruit is retained on the stalks.

Gather them quite dry, cut them off the stalks into clean dry bottles, filled close, but not to bruise them; cork and resin them over & set them in a fish kettle with cold water over a slow fire, to simmer very gently fifteen minutes, sit them off in the water till cold, then wipe the bottles dry, & keep them in a dry cupboard.

Currants, black, red or white

Pack the fruit close in a preserving bottle, top up with cold water adding the tops but not screwing down tightly. Place in enough water to come up above the neck of the bottle. Simmer for about 1½ hours. Remove and leave to cool and then slightly tighten the tops. Test the seals after 48 hours by removing the screw band and checking that the actual seals are still tight. Store in a dry, cool and, if possible, dark place.

DRINKS

CLARIFIED LEMONADE

Lemonade was a very popular drink thought suitable for ladies and children and a popular item on a picnic. There are 2 recipes in the collection, this one including milk. Mrs Rundell includes 4 recipes in her work, one for invalids and another which also includes boiled milk. Interestingly Grimley in his collection of Victorian recipes has one for a lemon brandy which includes brandy and milk in a recipe which directs the cook to let the mixture stand for eight days prior to bottling!

Take the rind of 4 Lemons & 11oz. of Loaf Sugar pour a quart of boiling Water on them take the juice of the 4 Lemons in a vefsel and pour a pint of boiling skim Milk upon it, let all remain so till the next Day then mix all together and add half a pint of White Wine, strain it thro' a linen bag till quite clear.

---

2 large lemons, rinds and juice
5½oz (160g) sugar
1 pint (570ml) boiling water
½ pint (275ml) skimmed milk
¼ pint (150ml) white wine, medium sweet

Pour the water over the lemon rind and sugar, the milk over the lemon juice and leave them to infuse overnight. The next day mix these together and add the wine. Strain the liquid through a muslin lined sieve and chill thoroughly before serving.

LEMONADE

The following recipe makes a more typical and excellent lemonade.

----

8 lemons pared squeeze the juice on the rind, leave it an hour then put in a pd & half of Lump sugar & two quarts of spring water When the sugar is melted strain it.

----

8 lemons, rind and juice
1½ lb (700g) sugar
4 pints (2.25litres) water

Place all the ingredients in a pan and heat gently until the sugar has melted. Leave to infuse for an hour or so then strain the liquid. Serve chilled.

GINGER WINE

Wine making was a further culinary skill of our Victorian forebears and the collection contains recipes for cowslip and ginger wines. The household inventory for William Wilshere who died in 1824 does in fact refer to 215 'Sundry Home made wines'. Ginger wine and beer, like lemonade, were popular Victorian drinks. I have included two of the Wilshere examples, the second purely for interest's sake. The following recipe makes a dry and rather potent drink which does benefit from being kept for a few weeks before opening. The original recipe included egg whites which would have been used to clean the sugar not so refined as our product. I must confess that I found the original recipe confusing as regards its directions to use a 'cooler' and then to pour boiling water over the lemons. The description of the lemon rinds as 'coats', however, makes a memorable phrase!

Eight gallons of Water, seven pounds of loaf sugar, four oz. of common white ginger root cut small but not bruised; The whites of six Eggs well beat stir it all well together & set it on the fire let it boil twenty minutes put it into a Cooler, pour the liquor boiling upon the pulp of Eight Lemons cut very thin, let it stand till quite cold then put it into the Cask, take the coats quite clean off the eight lemons, cut them into slices, take out the Pips, put them into the Cask with half an oz. of Isinglafs a large spoonful of Yeast at the top, do not stir it but close the Cask the next day, bottle it in ten days.

---

1 gallon (4.5litres) water
1lb (450g) sugar
½ to 1oz (10 to 25g) root ginger, peeled and grated
1 lemon, peel and juice
Packet of all purpose wine yeast made up according to the sachet instructions

Stir everything together except for the lemon rind, juice and yeast. Simmer for 20 minutes. Cool before adding to the lemon juice and peel and pour into a demi-john. Add the yeast but do not stir it in. Leave to ferment for 5 to 7 days and then bottle. Leave for at least a month before opening.

GINGER WINE

The addition of brandy would surely elevate this wine and make it a suitable partner for the clarified lemonade recipe!

To make Ginger Wine - To ten Gallons of Water put near ¾ pound of common white Ginger beat very fine 12lb 2½ of loaf sugar the whites of eight Eggs & the peel of 10 lemons pared very thin be careful to take off the white part of the Lemon slice them & take out every pippin, mix the Water, Sugar & Eggs together, stirr it well, when it boils put in the Ginger, do not skim it after the Ginger is in let it boil 20 minutes pour it boiling hot on the lemons when it is nearly cold put it into the Cask, put in a spoonful or two of Yeast, let it stand 24 hours, then put in half an ounce of Isinglafs & Bottle of White Brandy.

Bring it up close & in a fortnight Bottle it.

INVALID'S PUDDING

Such recipes were typical of this type of household collection and often consist of bread and milk or some sort of chicken-stock based concoction, food thought nourishing whilst relatively bland. I'm sure I remember being given bread and milk on occasions. The inclusion of the wine in this recipe, however, probably did a lot to keep up the spirits!

Soak a large piece of the crumb of a loaf of bread in boiling new milk over night if in the morning the bread has soaked up all the milk, add more boiling milk to cover it __ Three hours before it is to be eaten take the bread from the milk, tie it up in a cloth and boil it in skimmed milk for 3 hours__ Serve it up with a generous spoon of butter, wine & sugar.

TO MAKE POMADE DIVINE

The following recipes have been included purely for interest's sake to show the versatility of our forebears who were both cooks and chemists.

Take of Beef Marrow one Pound 8½ well picked from the Bone & filaments, put it into an Earthen Vesil full of Spring water, change the Water twice a day for ten days together; then draw it off & put a pint of Rose Water to it, let it stand 24 hours, then put it into a thin cloth & drain it as dry as possible; Then add of Benjamin Storax Turpintine & Florentine Orris, of each one ounce; of Cinnamon 1oz: of Cloves 2 Dms of Powdered Nutmeg 2 Dms all these must be finely powdered & well mixed with the Marrow. then put it into a Pewter vesel well closed, that nothing can evaporate. suspend the vesil in a Copper of boiling water & let it boil for 3 hours without ceasing & have water ready to replenish that in the Copper that the Pewter vefsel may always be covered, when it has boiled for 3 hours put it through a fine muslin into small Pots you intend keeping it in but don't cover them till quite cold. NB This Pomade is good for a sore Breast or Bruise & is not the worse for keeping for many years.

LETTUCE GINGER

Take the stalk of White Coss Lettuce before it become too old or stringy cut it in small pieces blanch it in water for 2 or 3 days Make a thin syrup to a quart of which add 5oz. of Sliced Ginger when cold pour it upon the Lettuce Boil up the syrup every other day for a fortnight at the last make it thick and add some slices of Lemon & Orange Peel to it. The syrup will be required to be reduced or strengthened as found necessary.

COUGH MIXTURE

This recipe is one of the few untitled documents but includes a postscript explaining its use and extolling its many successes claiming, even, that it has been trialed and so is no common quack remedy!

Take two Pounds of Raisins, stone them & put them into three quarts of strong new Wort that has had no Hops in it __ Boil it till reduced to three Pints , or a Quart, then strain it and drink a Tea Cup of it first thing in a Morning, and the last thing at Night __ If this quantity should be found too opening, it may be lefsend in the taking, at Discretion__

This receipt is excellent for a Cough & Hoarsenefs and a Consumption; many Trials have been made with great succefs.

DR. HALIFAX FOR A COUGH

This and the following recipe are among the few that are actually signed presumably by a friend or acquaintance.

Boil half a Pint of Vinegar & half a pound of Honey together to the consistency of a syrup and add to it whilst hot one ounce of Polychrist salt & half an ounce of nitre Take a Table spoonful three times a day in a quarter of a Pint of Boiling water.

(Willard)

95

RECEIPT FOR THE AGUE

1oz Red Bark, 1 Table spoonfull Black Pepper 1 Table spoonful Coarse Sugar. 1 nutmeg grated, The above Ingredients to be made into an electuary with syrup of Poppies. It will require 2oz of the Poppies to mix it properly, 3 Table spoonfulls to be taken as soon as the fit is off. An Emetic should be previously given.

(Mrs Dyme)

TO DESTROY FLYS

No doubt the sugar serves to attract the insects to this liquid doom, more ecologically sound than a fly spray though I confess that I have not put it to the test.

To 1 pint of milk add a ¼ of a pd. of raw sugar & two ozs. of Ground pepper simmer the same together 8 or so minutes & leave it about in shallow vessels.

FOR GNAT BITES

Short and sweet and straight to the point!

Indigo & water to be dabd frequently.

POT POURRI

The first recipe for pot pourri pays tribute to the glories of a Victorian garden and gives us a fleeting idea of the horticultural delights that were once a feature of Hitchin's grander houses. The second recipe, somewhat more manageable, does, however, sound most fragrant.

Put into a large China Jar the following ingredients in layers with bag salt strewed between the layers : two pecks of damask roses, part in buds & part blooming, violets, orange flowers & jasmine, a handful of each, orris root sliced, benjamin, & storax, two ounces of each; a quarter of an ounce of musk; a quarter of a pound of angelica root sliced; a quart of the red parts of close gilly flowers; two handfuls of Lavender flowers; hay and laurel leaves, half a handful of each, three Seville oranges, stuck as ful of cloves as possible, dried in a cool oven and pounded; half a handful of knotted marjoram; and two handfuls of balm of Gilead dried. Cover all quite close. When the pot is uncovered the perfume is very fine.

A Quicker sort of Sweet Pot

Take three handfuls of orange flowers, three of gilly flowers, three of Damask Roses, one of knotted marjoram, one of Lemon thyme, six bay leaves, a handful of rosemary, one of myrtle, half one of mint, and one of Lavender, the rind of a Lemon, and a quarter of an ounce of cloves. Chop all & put them in layers with pounded bay salt between up to the top of the jar.

If all the ingredients cannot be got at once, put them in as you can get them, always throwing in salt with every new article.

TAKE 6 CARROTS, 4 HEADS OF CELERY, 8 LARGE ONIONS ...

TO WASH FLANNELS THE FIRST TIME

The first wash was obviously a vital one for the longevity of this item.

Put the flannel in a pail and pour boiling water upon them & let them remain till cold & wash them in as hot water as you can bear your hands never rinse them but mangle them before they are quite dry. a small quantity of powder blue in the water.

References

FOREWORD
1. Mrs Beeton, Beeton's Book of Household Management, preface.

CHAPTER 1
1. Anthony Foster, Market Town, p.4.
2. Patricia Hanks and Flavia Hodges, A Dictionary of Surnames, p.578.
3. Kenneth Cameron, English Place-Names, pp.185 & 217.
4. Doris Palmer, A Brief History of Welwyn and The Frythe, p.6.
5. Doris Palmer, op.cit., p.6.
6. Tony Rook, The Church of Saint Mary, Welwyn, Then & Now, p.1.
7. John Edwin Cussons, History of Hertfordshire, p.212.
8. Noël Farris, The Wymondleys, p.57.
9. Tony Rook, op.cit., p.12.
10. Tony Rook, op.cit., p.12.

CHAPTER 2
1. Francis Lucas, Hitchin Biography, (unpub.) p.812, Hitchin Museum.
2. Francis Lucas, op.cit., p.813.
3. Francis Lucas, op.cit., p.817.
4. Helen Poole and Alan Fleck, Old Hitchin, Portrait of an English Market Town, p.39.
5. Reginald Hine, History of Hawkins Russell Jones (unpub.) p.4, Hawkins Russell Jones.
6. Doris Palmer, op.cit., p.9.
7. Reginald Hine, op.cit., p.10.
8. Anthony Foster, op.cit., p.173.
9. Inventory of the estate of William Wilshere, 1824, summary of valuation, Hitchin Museum.
10. Anthony Foster, op.cit., p.173.
11. Francis Lucas, op.cit., p.814.
12. An Account of the Hitchin Charities from The Further Report of the Commissioners Appointed in Pursuance of an Act of Parliament, 1833, p.12/13.
13. W.Branch Johnson, Articles on Hertfordshire History, p.56.
14. Reginald Hine, op.cit., p.40.
15. Reginald Hine, op.cit., p.31.
16. William Lucas, "A Quaker Journal", vol.1, p.143.
17. Francis Lucas, op.cit., p.822.
18. Francis Lucas, op.cit., p.818.
19. Philip Basham, The Wilsheres in Hitchin, Hertfordshire Countryside, vol. 47, no.399, pp.18 & 36.
20. Francis Lucas, op.cit., p.820
21. Reginald Hine, op.cit., p.14.
22. Francis Lucas, op.cit., p.821.
23. Reginald Hine, op.cit., pp.11/12.
24. Francis Lucas, op.cit., p.830.

25.Doris Palmer, op.cit., pp.10/11.
26.Anthony Foster, op.cit. p.194.
27.Lawson Thompson scrapbook, vol.1A, p.2, Hitchin Museum.
28.Doris Palmer, op.cit., p.13.

CHAPTER 3
1. Sarah Freeman, Mutton and Oysters ; the Victorians and Their Food, p.13/14.
2. Charles Elmé Francatelli, A Plain Cookery Book for the Working Classes, p.11.
3. Sarah Freeman, op.cit., p.55.
4. Journal of the Reports of the Inspectors of Nuisances, August 9th. 1906, Hitchin Museum.
5. Journal of the Reports of the Inspectors of Nuisances, August 20th. 1907, Hitchin Museum.
6. J.C.Drummond & Anne Wilbraham, The Englishman's Food, p.334.

Bibliography

PERIOD RECIPES
ACWORTH , Margaretta : Margaretta Ackworth's Georgian Cookery Book : ed. Alice & Frank Prochaska : Pavillion Books 1987.
BEETON, Isabella : Beeton's Book of Household Management : Chancellor Press 1989.
BROWNE, Phyllis : A Year's Cookery : Cassell & Co. 1895
FARLEY, John : The London Art of Cookery 1807 : ed. Ann Haly : Southover Press 1988.
FRANCATELLI, Charles : A Plain Cookery Book for the Working Classes 1861 : Pryor Publications 1993.
GLASSE, Hannah : The Art of Cookery Made Plain and Easy : Prospect Books, 1983.
RUNDELL, Mrs. : Domestic Cookery : Milner & Sowerby, 1862.

EDITED COLLECTIONS OF PERIOD RECIPES
MCKENDRY, Maxime : Seven Hundred Years of English Cooking : Treasure Press, 1973.
BLACK, Maggie : Food and Cooking in Nineteenth Century Britain : Letts, 1977
GRIMLEY, Gordon : The Victorian Cookery Book : Abelard-Schumann, 1973.
HOPE, Annette : Londoners' Larder : Mainstream Publishing, 1990.

GENERAL COOKERY REFERENCE BOOKS
DAVIES, Jennifer : The Victorian Kitchen : BBC Books, 1989.
DAVID, Elizabeth : English Bread and Yeast Cookery : Penguin, 1979.
DRUMMOND, J.C. & WILBRAHAM, A. : The Englishman's Food : Pimlico Press, 1991.
FREEMAN, Sarah : Mutton and Oysters. The Victorians and Their Food : Gollancz, 1989.
HARTLEY , Dorothy : Food in England : Futura, 1985.
TANNAHILL, Reay : Food in History : Penguin, 1988.
WILSON, C.Anne : Food and Drink in Britain : Constable, 1991.

SOME SOURCES FOR INFORMATION ON HITCHIN AND THE WILSHERES
BASHAM, Philip : The Wilsheres in Hitchin : Hertfordshire Countryside, vol.47, no.399.
CUSSONS, John Edwin : History of Hertfordshire.
FARRIS, Noël : The Wymondleys : Hertfordshire Publications, 1989.
FIELD, Richard : Hitchin. A Pictorial History : Phillimore, 1991.
FOSTER, Anthony : Market Town : Hitchin Historical Society, 1987.
HINE, Reginald : Hitchin Worthies : Allen & Unwin, 1932.
PALMER, Doris : A Brief History of Welwyn and The Frythe : Smith Kline & French Research Institute, now SmithKline Beecham.
POOLE, Helen and FLECK, Alan : Old Hitchin, Portrait of an English Market Town. From the Cameras of T.B.Latchmore and others. Eric T Moore in association with North Hertfordshire Museums, 1976.

List of Illustrations

INDEX TO RECIPES

List of Subscribers

J Aitchison
Mrs Jennifer Alder
Mrs H J Allison
Jean Anderson
Helen Ansell
Mr & Mrs Barry Arends
R S Ashwood
Adrian & Alison Bagg
Marjorie Barrow
Mrs Johanna Barter
Gwen Bartlett
Bernard & Nona Blay
Mrs Stella Bousfield
Wendy Bowker
M Bradbeer
Mr Stephen Bradford-Best
Mrs M Bradshaw
L J Brodie
S Brown
Cyril B C Buck
Mrs P S Bunker
Mrs Dorothy Cain
Hilary F Cannon
Mr G F J Caple
Mrs S N Carey
Carole Carter
Mrs H R Carver
Miss M Cave
Mrs P Chappelle
Lynne Cheetham
Mrs J Clark
Ellie Clarke
Lesley & David Clarke
Peter & Leslie Collett
Elisabeth Compton
Barbara Cook
Mrs I Cornelius
Ann Crook
Catherine M Davis
Christa R Dawson
Ida Doolan
Mr M E Doughty
Priscilla Douglas

Sue Durham
Zoë Embleton
Mrs Exton Jones
Mrs Lucy Farley
Mr & Mrs P J Farmer
Tim Farr
Sue Fisher
S R Fisher
W J & J Fisher
Clare & Alan Fleck
Ms S M Fletcher
Mrs F M Fleck
Mr David Fosdike
Mr & Mrs R F Foster
Mrs G Foulkes
Miss J Gabriel
Mrs D Gibson
G A Goodman
The Gouldstone Family
Mr R I C Gray
Mrs Audrey Green
Halsey & Son
Mr & Mrs Harmer
A H Harris
P E Hartley
Hawkins Russell Jones
William Heaton
Hertfordshire Library Service
Hertfordshire Local Studies Service
Mrs Ann Heymans
Joy Hillman
Mrs Cynthia Hindmarch
Hitchin Girls School
Mrs K A Howard
Mrs E Howarth
David & Bridget Howlett
Ruth Howroyd
Chris & Trina Hubbard
L E & D Hughes
Pauline Humphries
Bridget Hunt
Ms Liz Hunter
Mrs C A Iley

Take 6 Carrots, 4 Heads of Celery and 8 Large Onions ...

Kathleen Kazer
T F Knight
Mr & Mrs Lang
Doreen Leuty
Brian Limbrick
Alan Lintern
Mrs Victoria Lockyer
Mrs Frances Maciver
Mrs Rachel MacKenzie
John Mahoney
Mrs Ethel Manning
Zoë Martin
Leslie & Pamela Maunders
Miss C A Mills
Mrs Barbara Mitchell
Mrs Pansy Mitchell
Tracy Moralee
Annabel Morgan
Mrs M A Morgan
Mrs S Morgan
Mr & Mrs D Mortimer
Mrs Joyce Musson
Howard & Jinty Nelson
Dr G R Parish
Graeme & Sian Parkin
Mr & Mrs J D Parkins
Mr & Mrs Payne
Miss S Payne
Mrs Jean Peach

Grace Peters
Miss K Petrie
Mrs P M D Pieris
Richard Reason
Mrs Elizabeth Rose
Mary Rutherford
Carol Samples
Mr P G Saunders
Mrs P E Sim
Pam & Ray Skeggs
Julie Skinner
Mrs Margaret Schmierer
Mrs B J Smith
Miss K E Stokes
Janet Swan
Mr B Tarry
Alison Taylor
Rachel Thomson
Linda & Adrian Tobey
Mrs K M Tookey
Mrs Ruth W Turner
Joan Underhill
D R Walmsley
Mrs N W Wheeler
Helen Wicks
Dr & Mrs J R B Williams
Mr R D Wisbey
W Wolstencroft

Wilshere Family Tree
from John Edwin Cussons, History of Hertfordshire

Elizabeth, bap. 25 Apr. 1605; mar. 23rd Oct. 1628; ob. 9th Oct. 1691 = Richard Meade, bur. 5th October 1661

Anne, bap. 5th March, 1606-7; bur. 18th February, 1656-7

John, bap. 8th Janry. 1608-9; ob.s.p. 10 of June, 1635 (Inq. p. mort. 11 Car. 1)

Thomas, of South Wootton, Co. Norfolk; bap. 6 Mar. 1610-11; ob. June, 1666; will dated 7 Aug. 1666; proved 24th May, 1667 (P.C.C.) = Margaret, da. and coh. of Thos. Williamson, of Reading; Extrix. of her husband's will; ob. at St. Albans; bur. 3 March, 1678-9

Joane, bap. 24th Jan. 1612-3; bur. 22nd Oct. 1639; unmarried

John, bap. 5th Mar. 1628-9 — Anne, bap. 5 Jan. 1630-1 — Elizabeth, bap. 26 Dec. 1639

Thomas, bap. 15 May, 1636 — George, bap. 10 Sept. 1637 — Samuel, bap. 22 Feb. 1638-9

Joseph, bap. 29 Aug. 1641 — Richard, bap. 5 Aug. 1643 — Lettice, bap. 9 Nov. 1645; bur. 5 Mar. 1647

Gilbert, bap. 5 July, 1651; bur. 16 July, 1661 — John, bap. 15 June, 1653

Elizabeth, bap. 7 July, 1608 — Susan, bap. 17 May, 1615

Margaret, bap. 3 Oct. 1644; bur. 8 March, 1646 — Hester, bap. 3rd July, 1646

Richard, bap. 17th Septemb. 1648; bur. 12th Oct. 1651

Thomas, ob. unm. bur. 19th February, 1669-70

Ann Ireland, 1st wife; bur. 26 June, 1684 = John, bap. 24th Sept. 1645; bur. 14th Oct. 1741 = Dorothy, da. of William Whitbread, of Cardington, Co. Bedford; m. 1686

Zachariah, bap. 22 Nov. 1647; bur. 29th Nov. 1647

Margaret, bap. 20th Dec. 1648

Elizabeth, bap. 19th Apr. 1651 = John Parsons, of Wallingford, County Berks

Ann, bap. 29 March, 1653; bur. 18 Feb. 1656-7

Richard, bap. 27 Novemb. 1655

Joseph, bap. 5th January, 1659-60 — Ann, bap. in London 15 Aug. 1663

Dorothy, bap. 5th Dec. 1688 = James Amory 1st husband

William Miles, 1st husband = Lettice = John Inkersole, 2nd husband

Martha, bap. 13 Mar. 1692 = John Kentish

Alice, bap. 27th Aug. 1693 = Robert Berry

John, bap. and buried in parish of St. Andrew, Undershaft, London, 1696

William, bap. 2 July, 1700; ob. 15, bur. 20th October, 1786 = Sarah, da. and coh. of Wm. Seeling: m. May, 1729, ob. 20 Mar. 1792

William Wilshere, of the Frythe, born 5th April, 1730; mar. 22 Sept. 1753, ob. 1 Nov. 1758 = Susanna, da. of Simon and Susanna Browne, ob. 12th February, 1800, aged 66

Sarah, m. = George Haynes 1752

William, b. 6 Sept. 1754, F.A.S., Lieut. Colonel of Local Militia; Chairman of Quarter Sessions for Beds; ob.s.p. 2 September, 1824 = Martha, 3rd da. of Hale Wortham, of Royston, ob. 8 Sept. 1786

Sarah Kimpton, 1st wife; ob. 29th Sept. 1781, aged 24 — Arabella, da. Francis Hawkins, clerk, Rect. of Higham Gobion, Co. Beds; 3rd wife, ob. 1st Feb. 1816, in her 58th year

John, b. 25 Oct. 1755, ob. 21 Oct. 1836 = Mary Prentice; 2nd wife; ob. 14 June, 1794, aged 45

Sarah, b. 7 June, 1757, ob. 22 Oct. 1773 — Susanna, b. 29th Dec. 1758, ob. 23 June, 1774

Martha, b. 10th Jan. 1760, ob. 30th Sept. 1774 — George, b. 16th Jan. 1761, ob. an infant

Elizabeth, b. 14th March, 1762, ob. 11 March, 1775 — Simon, b. 8 July, 1763, ob. 4th Oct. 1789

James, b. 21 Aug. 1765; d. an infant — Ann, b. 30 Oct. 1766, ob. 31st March, 1843

Mary, b. 8 May, 1768, ob. 26 Sep. 1861 — James, b. 26th Sept. 1769, ob. an infant

James, b. 25 Feb. 1771, ob. 19 July, 1799, s.p. = Alice Long — Frances, b. 18th Nov. 1772, ob. 1 Feb. 1774

Thomas Wilshere, of The Frythe, 15th child, b. 27th Feb. 1775; Capt. Local Militia, ob. 1st Sept. 1832 = Lora, da. of Charles Beaumont, b. 20th Sept. 1775, ob. 13 June, 1846

Thomas Hailey = Elizabeth, ob.s.p. 4 Dec. 1863, aged 80

William, ob.s.p. 15 Oct. 1853, aged 68 = Louisa Croft; living 1877

William Wilshere, of The Frythe, b. 28 July, 1804; M.P. for Great Yarmouth 1837-47; High Sheriff 1858, ob. cœleb. 10th Nov. 1867

Laura-Beaumont, b. 31 Dec. 1806, ob. 29 July, 1859 = Thomas Mills, Deputy Chairman Quarter Sessions for Herts; M.P. for Totnes; b. 18 Oct. 1794, ob. 10 November, 1862, s.p.

Elizabeth-Simpson, b. 13 July, 1808, ob. 3 Feb. 1812

Thomas, b. 28th Jan. 1811, ob. unmarried 13th Sept. 1840

Charles-Willes Wilshere, of The Frythe, b. 20 Feb. 1814; m. 25th Aug. 1840, at Munich, in Germany; living 1877 = Elisabeth-Marie, da. of W. M. Farmer, of Nonsuch, Co. Surrey; M.P. for Huntingdon; born 8 April, 1810; living 1877

Edith-Elisabeth-Marie, born 27 July, 1841, at Chester St., Grosvenor Place, London; living unmarried 1877

Everilda-Frances-Laura, born 7th June, 1846, at St. James's Place, London; living unmar. 1877

Florence, born at Florence 31 Jan. 1848, mar. 29 July, 1869, at Christ Church, Albany Street, London; living 1877 = Guilbert-Edward-Wyndham, eldest son of Rev. William-Wyndham Malet, Vicar of Ardeley, Co. Hertford; born 12 July, 1839; Captain R.H. Artillery; living 1877

Alice-Augusta, born 4 May, 1850, at Hitchin, Co. Hertford; living unmarried 1877

PEDIGREE OF THE FAMILY OF WILSHERE.

On a slab in the chancel of Welwyn Church to Richard Meade and Elizabeth, his wife (née Wilshere), dated 14th May, 1700, it is stated that 'this hath been the burying place of the said Mrs. Meade's Ancestours, the Wilshers, for Three Hundred Years last past.' William Wylshere, who died in 1558, desired by his will to be buried "in the chancel of the parryshe church of Wellwyne whereat the sepulture doth stand." This clearly indicates that at that time there was a family tomb or monument in the chancel. When the church was restored in 1869-70, several stones, from which the brasses had long since been taken, were removed from the chancel and nave. One had commemorated a husband, his wife, and several children. These, or some of them, may have been to members of the family of Wilshere, but there is no evidence to prove it.

The first four generations in the subjoined Pedigree are, to some extent, conjectural. Preserved in the muniment room at the Frythe, is an immense number of old family deeds, and among these are several which clearly prove that from the time of Richard II. until the end of the reign of Queen Mary, the Wilsheres were large resident landowners in Welwyn. They, however, all bear but one of two Christian names—William or John : the individuality of each is therefore difficult to determine. It is to be presumed that the property descended in lineal succession, but there is no proof that the first John whom I make to be the son of William and Edith, was not the brother, grandson, or nephew of his predecessor. From the second John, who married Elizabeth, the Pedigree may be relied on as being absolutely correct.

William Wylshere, settled at the Frythe, als Frythe Hall, in Welwyn, Co. Hertford, temp. Ric. II. = . . .

William Wylshere, of the Frythe, temp. Ric. II., Hen. IV., V., and VI. = Edith

John Wylshere, of the Frythe, temp. Edw. IV. and Hen. VII. = Isabella Langley

John Wylshere, temp. Hen. VII. and VIII. = Elizabeth, bur. 11 Jan. 1558-9

Cicely ; 1st wife = William Wylshere, purchased the Manor and Advowson of the Rectory of Welwyn, and other estates, parcel of the = Joan, 2nd wife ; possessions of the dissolved Priory of Halliwell, in Middlesex. Ob. 15, bur. 17 Nov. 1558, "in the chancel of buried 1st Oct. the parryshe church of Wellwyne, whereat the sepulture doth stand." Will proved 3rd March, 1558-9 (P.C.C.) 1560

Thomas, of Willian ; buried in Willian = Elizabeth Church ; will dated 23 Feb. 1539-40 ; proved 16 June, 1540 (Archd. Hunts)

Alice = Thomas Wylshere, held the Frythe by Licence of Alienation from his father, dat. 3 Edw. VI., ob. 15 May, 1570 (Inq. p. m. 14 Apr. 16 Eliz.)

Richard   William   John = . . .   Thomas, of the parish of = Jane, to whom administration Christ Church, London   of late husband's goods was granted 6th August, 1590

James   Robert

Thomas Wylshere, aged 21, 14 April, 16 Eliz. ; ob. 18, = Joan Battyl, of Digswell, da. of William and Johan Battyl, of Digswell bur. 21 Mar. 1620-1 ; will dated 12 March, 1620-1 ; (see brass in church there) ; mar. 21 July, 1572 ; buried 1 May, 1622 ; proved 28 March ,1621 (Archd. Hunts) will dated 23 April, 1622 ; proved 4 March, 1622-3 (Archd. Hunts)

Cicelye   Ann, mar. 3 = William Field, bur. Nov. 1577 | 28th Feb. 1612-3

Johane

Annys = John Wilshere, bap. Sanders, 7 Dec. 1574 ; rated m.12 Oct. in terrâ in Subsidy 1603, bur. Roll 1 Chas. I. at 40s. 29 Sept. sold manor and adv. 1632 of church to All Souls College, Oxford ; bur. 26 July, 1646

Frances Man- = Thomas, bap. 21 nestve, mar. at Jan. 1576-7 ; in- Datchworth, stituted to Rect. 14 Dec. 1608 ; of Welwyn 16th bur. 12 June, June, 1606 ; ob. 1610 ; 1st wife 10, bur. 16 June, 1651

Elizabeth Smyth, m. at Steeple Morden, 10 June, 1611 ; 2nd wife

George, of Welwyn, bap. = Lettice, 17 Sept. 1578 ; rated in bur. 7th terrâ in Subsidy Roll 1 Novbr. Chas. I. at 20s. ; bur. 13 1657 Oct. 1634 ; will dated 1 Sept. 1634 ; proved 4 Nov. 1634 (Archd. Hunts)

William, of Stevenage ; bapt. 16th Apr. 1581

Ann, bap. = Michael 31st Jan. Squire, 1583 ; m. exor. of 29 May, J o a n 1605 W i l - shere's will

Robert, bap. 12 S e p t. 1585 ; bur. 1st J u l y, 1586

Jasper, of Caxton, Co.Camb. bap. 10th July, 1588

Joane, = William Battell, bap. 20 her cousin ; exor. J u l y, of Joan Wil- 1589 shere's will 1623

Anne, = William bapt. 14 Norman- J a n r y. ton 1609-10, mar. 27 Decbr. 1627

William, bap. 25th Oct.1612, ob. an in- fant — Henry, bap. 12th March, 1613-14 ; bur. 1 Ap. 1614

Mary, bap. 10 A u g. 1615 — Eliza- beth, bap. 17 Novbr. 1616 ; bur. 4 Decbr. 1616

Thomas, bap. 14 J u n e, 1618 — George, bap. 8th April, 1 6 1 9 ; Rector of Great Ayot

Elizabeth, bap. 9 Oct. 1620 — Robert, bap. 13th Oct. 1622 ; bur. 17th Feb. 1623

Jasper, bap. 10 October, 1624 — Frances, bap. 12 April, 1 6 2 7 ; bur. 30 March, 1629

Frances, bap. 7th October, 1629 — Richard, bap. 9th Decbr. 1632

Thomas, bap. 5th October, 1 6 0 6 ; bur. 27 M a y, 1634

Lettice, = Thomas bap. 6th Bassett, October, widower 1511 ; m. 10 Nov. 1634

George, bap. 16 October, 1614 — John, bap. 16 March, 1616-7 ; bur. 26 Febry. 1646-7

J o a n, bap. 18 J u n e, 1620 — Thomas, bap. 8th J u n e, 1623

Edward, bap. 20 M a y, 1 6 2 7 ; bur. 20 J u n e, 1627 — Jasper, bap. 20 M a y, 1627

Joan, bp. 25 June, 1606 — Michael, bap. 26 J u n e, 1608

Arthure, = . . . bap. 20 Septem- ber 1584

Mary, bap. 5 Apr. 1579 — Mary, bap. 19th June, 1580 — Alice, bap. 7 Apr. 1583

Thomas, Samuel, bap. 5th Decbr. 1608
John, bap. 16 March, 1616-7 ; bur. 26 Febry. 1646-7